SEA TURTLES

An Extraordinary Natural History of Some Uncommon Turtles

For Dawn

Photography © 2006 by:

Front cover © Masa Ushioda/SeaPics.com
Back cover © François Gohier
Page 1 © NHPA/Kevin Schafer
Page 3 © NHPA/Linda Pitkin
Page 4 © Masa Ushioda/SeaPics.com
Page 6 © Colin Baxter
Page 7 © Reinhard Dirscherl/SeaPics.com
Page 8 © James D Watt/SeaPics.com
Page 9 © Masa Ushioda/SeaPics.com
Page 10 © Kelly Spranger/V&W/SeaPics.com
Page 11 © SA Team/Foto Natura/Minden Pictures
Page 12 © Doug Perrine/SeaPics.com
Page 13 © Doug Perrine/SeaPics.com
Page 14 © Masa Ushioda/SeaPics.com
Page 16 © Colin Baxter
Page 17 © Douglas David Seifert/ardea.com
Page 18 © Reinhard Dirscherl/SeaPics.com
Page 19 © Colin Baxter
Page 21 © Doug Perrine/naturepl.com
Page 22 © Andre Seale/SeaPics.com
Page 23 © Jeff Rotman/naturepl.com
Page 25 © Colin Baxter
Page 26 © David B Fleetham/SeaPics.com
Page 28 top © Doug Perrine/SeaPics.com
Page 28 bottom © Doug Perrine/SeaPics.com
Page 30 left © Tom Walmsley/Splashdown Direct
Page 30 right © Ben Osborne/naturepl.com
Page 31 © Mike Parry/Minden Pictures
Page 33 © Mark Conlin/SeaPics.com
Page 34 © Ben Osborne/naturepl.com
Page 37 © NHPA/Jany Sauvanet

Page 38 © NHPA/Kevin Schafer
Page 39 © Steve Winter/National Geographic Image Collection
Page 40 © NHPA/Kevin Schafer
Page 41 © Pat de La Harpe/naturepl.com
Page 42 © Gerry Ellis/Minden Pictures
Page 44 © Valerie Taylor/ardea.com
Page 45 left © Doug Perrine/SeaPics.com
Page 45 right © Doug Perrine/SeaPics.com
Page 47 © Doug Perrine/SeaPics.com
Page 49 © Lisa Steiner/SeaPics.com
Page 50 © Doug Perrine/SeaPics.com
Page 52 © Tom & Pat Leeson
Page 55 © Jez Tryner/SeaPics.com
Page 56 © Doug Perrine/SeaPics.com
Page 59 © Jurgen Freund/naturepl.com
Page 60 © Colin Baxter
Page 61 © Gavin Parsons/ardea.com
Page 63 © Michael Patrick O'Neill/SeaPics.com
Page 64 © Mark Strickland/SeaPics.com
Page 65 © Walt Stearns/SeaPics.com
Page 66 © Amar Guillen/SeaPics.com
Page 67 © Jez Tryner/SeaPics.com
Page 71 © Norbert Wu/Minden Pictures
Page 73 © Valerie Taylor/ardea.com
Page 74 © Doug Perrine/SeaPics.com
Page 76 © Valerie Taylor/ardea.com
Page 77 © Valerie Taylor/ardea.com
Page 80 © Peter Steyn/ardea.com
Page 82 © Doug Perrine/SeaPics.com
Page 84 © Norbert Wu/Minden Pictures
Page 85 © Flip Nicklin/Minden Pictures

Page 88 © Robert van Dam
Page 90 © Colin Baxter
Page 91 © Norbert Wu/Minden Pictures
Page 92 © Robert van Dam
Page 93 © Colin Baxter
Page 97 © Doug Perrine/SeaPics.com
Page 98 © Frans Lanting/Minden Pictures
Page 100 © Tim Martin/naturepl.com
Page 101 © François Gohier
Page 105 © Doug Perrine/SeaPics.com
Page 106 © Pieter Pritchard/SeaPics.com
Page 107 © Doug Perrine/SeaPics.com
Page 108 © Anne Heimann
Page 109 © Doug Perrine/SeaPics.com
Page 113 © Ben Osborne/naturepl.com
Page 114 © Ben Osborne/naturepl.com
Page 115 © Jean-Paul Ferrero/Auscape/Minden Pictures
Page 119 © Rowan Byrne/SeaPics.com
Page 120 © Karik Shanker
Page 122 © Doug Perrine/SeaPics.com
Page 123 © Doug Perrine/naturepl.com
Page 124 © Patricio Robles Gil/Sierra Madre/Minden Pictures
Page 126 © Gavin Parsons/ardea.com
Page 127 top © Colin Baxter
Page 127 bottom © Colin Baxter
Page 128 top © M. Watson/ardea.com
Page 128 bottom © M. Watson/ardea.com
Page 129 © Anne Heimann
Page 130 © Ben Osborne/naturepl.com
Page 131 © Jurgen Freund/naturepl.com

Front Cover: *A green turtle near Kona, Hawaii.*   Back Cover: *A basking green turtle.*
Page 1: *A green turtle hatchling departs Ascension Island.*   Page 3: *A green turtle off Maui, Hawaii.*

Printed in China

SEA TURTLES

An Extraordinary Natural History of Some Uncommon Turtles

Blair Witherington

Contents

A Caribbean hawksbill turtle glides by a colorful tapestry of sponges lining Bloody Bay Wall, Cayman Islands.

Sea Turtles

Some may find it difficult to imagine a turtle with the elegance of a bird. It is a conception that seems to surpass the broadly accepted turtle quintessence – that of a plodding reptilian beast, hardened by millennia into a rigidly built, sluggish, almost rock-like form. But this description overlooks many turtles, and it is perhaps least representative of the group of creatures I introduce here – the sea turtles. They are indeed ancient. But throughout those millions of years of life on Earth, epochs before birds ever flew, sea turtles have glided with fluid form through their gossamer world, leaving the stereotypical turtle far behind. As a group, the sea turtles have acquired the shapes of animals inspired by the oceans challenges. They are dynamic, graceful, and capable of astounding athletic feats. Sea turtles are animals consummately at home in the sea, and they are truly elegant.

Before I first encountered sea turtles in their element, I had my own preconceived notions about how they should behave. I was a college student visiting a friend in the Virgin Islands, an archipelago dotting the northeastern rim of the Caribbean Sea. At the time I was developing an interest in herps, that is, reptiles and amphibians, a related grouping of scaly or moist-skinned animals that tend to crawl on their bellies.

As a budding herpetologist, my sea turtle preconception came mostly from general accounts of their nesting. Sea turtles, I learned from limited descriptions, were marine reptiles inextricably tied to the land for their reproduction. Thus, a female sea turtle gravid with eggs is driven to leave her familiar element, drag herself above the tide, and struggle through a series of critical steps associated with burying and hiding her eggs. There on land, an intimate process is

acted out where any uninitiated observer can sit closely by, watch, and take notes. In popular accounts especially, there is often an emphasis on the apparent tribulation of the turtle's task. The female's bulk, gravity, and human empathy being what they are, many observers convince the reader that sea turtles

A green turtle glides downward within the clear Celebes Sea off Borneo.

suffer the fate of most large reptiles – a life of stalwart, slow-paced responses to adversity.

I had hoped to see the turtles that grazed the seagrass pastures off St. John. So, slipping with mask and snorkel into the vividly clear Caribbean, I kicked out from one of the island's rocky cove beaches, beyond the bare coralline sand and toward broader waters. After only a few minutes I was hovering over the lush seagrass beds common in the

Sea turtles 'fly' using their wing-like flippers and are surprisingly swift at sea.

shallows surrounding the Virgin Islands. It was a serene place where slowly waving green ribbons of turtle grass (*Thalassia*) pointed out the gentle flow toward a bright teal backdrop. There in the filtered distance, creatures faded into view· that would substantially alter my impression of the reptilian lot in life.

The sunburst shell coloration of a green turtle contrasts with the silvery reflections of swimming jacks.

They were green turtles... three of them. Each of their shells was a brilliant teardrop as broad as my own torso and patterned with seabottom sunbursts. Their forelimbs were tapered wings that paused with graceful hesitation between beats, punctuating an underwater flight that seemed effortless. I had drifted into their path, and in formation, the three turtles glided around me, making a complete circle with a cautious radius and presenting me the greatest breadth of their shells. Each streamlined head was turned

so that I could be closely examined. In excitement, I found myself kicking toward them, but the distance between us held constant, no matter how vigorously I struggled to close the gap. Gliding through their wide orbit, the turtles angled their backs and eyes to me while they calmly, cautiously, surveyed the gawking alien. Then, each turtle banked away, and with a few rapid flaps, they dissolved into their world.

My first swim with sea turtles changed my notions about them and presented me with a view of these animals that persists still. To me, sea turtles are beautiful and intriguing creatures that tease us with a contrast of both accessibility and mystery. It is a view shared by a tightly knit group of people who are committed to learning ever more about sea turtles and their world. Biologists find their study of sea turtles benefiting from the way that these fascinating animals present themselves to us, and recently, our understanding about the lives of sea turtles has broadened greatly. Yet, many deep and provocative secrets seem to remain just out of reach.

I hope that this book will provide an appropriate portrait of our seven species of living sea turtles. It has neither the depth nor the detail of a complete description of their biology. Rather, it is an introduction. The overture seems fitting for the familiarity needed to begin a healthy relationship. The book begins with descriptions of how sea turtles go about their lives, and ends with a look at the connections between sea turtles and humans. For, as enigmatic and distant from us as sea turtles seem to be, clues continually arise describing how our lives are intertwined.

Blair Witherington

*Hawaiian green turtles at a 'cleaning station' submit to the
attentions of tangs. This symbiotic reciprocity, exchanging food for cleanliness,
is but one of many ecological links between sea turtles and their world.*

Ancient Origins

Sea turtles were shaped on a planet that we would barely recognize as our own. The splendid peak of experimentalism in sea turtle species was a time when more than 30 forms plied Earth's oceans. It was a time when a proto-Atlantic was just broadening with volcanic fits and starts between a splitting Gondwana super-continent. It was roughly 75 million years before human beings walked upright, the island India was still separated from Eurasia by a vast ocean, most of Europe was under water, flowering plants were a novel introduction to the world, and a diverse radiation of dinosaurs enjoyed their dominance on land. The Atlantic Ocean of this Cretaceous-period world was a thin seaway that snaked between the Americas and Africa, and at its northern extent, a rich, shallow Niobrara Sea covered the center of North America east of the Rocky Mountains. In this sea swam *Archelon ischyros*, an immense sea turtle named with Greek roots for primitive turtle and strength.

Archelon was indeed robust: 15 ft (4.5 m) in length, flippers spanning well over 16 ft (5 m), a 3 ft (1m) long head more than 2 ft (0.5 m) wide, and a weight of roughly 4850 lb (2200 kg). It was a turtle more massive than many modern automobiles, and its home included the sunlit sea that once covered South Dakota. There, the enormous turtle pursued equally monstrous Cretaceous squid, seizing them with its powerful curved beak. This great turtle bore the stiff, wing-like fore-flippers and smooth hydrodynamic form of modern sea turtles, but differed enough to be categorized in a separate family from what may be the closest living *Archelon* relative, the leatherback turtle (*Dermochelys coriacea*).

Both *Archelon* and the leatherback share characters that include an incompletely boned shell and relatively rapid growth, the latter trait indicated by the vascular, blood-rich growing ends of their long bones. *Archelon* may well have been a highly specialized turtle with narrow food tastes and parochial habits. As a specialist, *Archelon* would have had trouble coping with the cataclysmic world changes that took place during the late Cretaceous, changes that obliterated the once wildly

The leatherback turtle, a survivor of many cataclysmic world events occurring over millions of years, is now facing extinction.

successful dinosaurs, many other large vertebrates, and every other marine reptile except for our present-day sea turtles and one marine crocodile.

As old as *Archelon* seems, the origins of sea turtles lie much deeper. As a group, turtles have persisted with their distinctive shelled form since the Triassic Period, 210 million years before present. Their appearance predates the dinosaurs by just a few million years. The earliest known turtle, *Proganochelys* (new Latin

Sea turtles similar to this hawksbill have been around for about 100 million years.

for brilliant turtle-predecessor) lived in marshy areas but was not specialized for purely aquatic life. The truest marine-adapted turtles would not appear for another 10 to 50 million years or so, during the Jurassic Period, when members of two distinct turtle families (Pleurosternidae and Thalassemyidae) began to live in the shallow seas covering Europe. But these turtles did not leave the sea turtle descendants we know today. These earliest sea turtles

Ancient Hawaiian petroglyphs (rock carvings) depict honu, the green turtle, symbol of creation, longevity, prosperity, and wisdom.

had only partially modified limbs for stroking in shallow waters and disappeared before the most recent trials with ocean living took place in the Cretaceous.

The Cretaceous was the heyday for sea turtles, and all of the sea turtle species we know today have their roots in this period. Between 110 and 65 million years ago there were dozens of species varying among four (or by some opinions, three) families:

Toxochelyidae: Sea turtles in this family had circular or broad, heart-shaped shells. They last swam 30-50 million years ago, but these turtles may belong with the hard-shelled sea turtles alive today, the cheloniids.

Protostegidae: This family of *Archelon* included other large turtles. Each had a partially boned shell with distinct keels. Protostegid sea turtles last swam roughly 60 million years ago and may have been snuffed out by the same asteroid that led to the demise of the dinosaurs.

Dermochelyidae: Turtles of this family are not well represented by fossils and some species are known only from bits and pieces. There is a single species living today, the leatherback. Members of this family have shells that are a mosaic of bony elements rather than a solid covering of interconnected bone. In the leatherback we see that this carapace of composite bone and connective tissue is covered with thick skin. The leatherback's family is linked to the family of *Archelon*, the protostegids.

Cheloniidae: These are the thecate or hard-shelled sea turtles. Six species survive today and each has a bony carapace covered with thin skin protected by broad plates of keratin. Our living cheloniid sea turtles are probably more generalized and more coastal than many of the specialized oceanic forms that are no longer with us.

The sea turtles of today probably had a single common Cretaceous ancestor, but the evidence of this forebear has yet to be uncovered. At one time, the sea turtles were not considered a 'natural' grouping because of the highly variant form seen in the leatherback. However, ancestral trees developed from both DNA similarities and from the appearance of unique physical structures affirm that leatherbacks are more closely related to other sea turtles than to other turtles in general.

Six of the seven species of modern sea turtles have a hard shell and are grouped together in the same family. Sea turtles were formerly more diverse, having four families and dozens of species.

Form and Function

The Essence of Being Turtle

We are at least a little bit like turtles. Both turtles and we have four limbs, bound by bony girdles to a column of vertebrae ending in a neck that bears a prominent skull and movable jaws. We both are vertebrate animals. But among the vertebrates, turtles deserve awards for some of the most creative and bizarre uses of a skeleton.

The bizarre creativity of turtles is to be able to hide within their own bony, thoracic framework (their ribcage). In chelonians, thoracic bones and skin coverings have evolved into turtle armor – a tough shell that protects most or all of the indispensable parts of a turtle. In some species, everything that could be chewed on by a predator can be withdrawn into the shell, but in sea turtles, head, limbs, and tail remain outside. The basic elements of a turtle's shell are the bony carapace (upper shell), sheathed in skin that is completely covered by tough keratinized plates or scutes in most turtles, and the slightly less bony plastron (lower shell), which is also generally covered in scutes. Roughly 50 sutured bones make up the carapace of most turtles and nine bones form the plastron. In the shell of most adult turtles, spine, ribs and carapace bones are fused, and connect to the plastron to form a rigid box.

To know a turtle's shell is to know their life strategy – their method of survival that has persisted through millions of years of predator evolution. The difficulty in cracking that tough shell has protected turtles from most predators, lengthened their lives as individuals, and has allowed a lifestyle that is the very model of conservatism. In many ways, the turtle's shell has allowed many of the other traits thought of as being 'typically turtle.' Turtles are generally described as being persistent in form, deliberate in behavior, late maturing, and long lived.

A turtle's shell is as unlikely as it has been influential. The development of a turtle's shell from garden-variety vertebrate parts involved some profound and innovative steps in evolution. For one, the girdles that support limb movement have been drawn into the ribcage. In this trick of utmost contortion, it is as if a broad thoracic 'umbrella' swallowed up the shoulders and hips, which are outside the ribs in a typical vertebrate. The ribs themselves can hardly be considered a cage, given that the spaces between the bars have filled in with thick dermal bone (different in origin from the ribs themselves). The dermal bone of the carapace begins in young turtles as a fusion that binds spine and ribs together into a rigid shield. Toward adulthood, this dermal bone grows outward between the ribs and out to their ends to meet a chain of marginal carapace bones at the edges of the shell. Beneath the carapace, dermal bones in the turtle's plastron grow outward and in some species join with the carapace.

Part of the uniqueness of sea turtles is in their modification of the archetypal turtle shell. The rigid box of fused bone has become too confining for sea turtles, and they have evolved a more flexible shell in which carapace and plastron are joined by a bridge of supple cartilage. In the hard-shelled sea turtles, the cheloniids, the adult carapace is mostly rigid and is covered with broad scutes that vary in thickness. Hawksbills are protected by tough, partially overlapping carapace plates as thick as a fiberglass boat hull, whereas flatbacks are so thinly covered that a human fingernail can scratch the shell down to bleeding skin. In the leatherback, bone in the shell has been reduced most of all, with the ribs broadened but separate, and dermal bone limited to hundreds of coin-like bony plates embedded beneath thick skin and connective tissue that covers the carapace.

Nearly all of a sea turtle's flipper is its hand: a wrist and long fingers within a wing-like web.

Sea turtles rise to the surface
to breathe every 20 minutes
or so, but a relaxed turtle may
remain submerged for hours.
Just before they reach the surface
they blow a cloud of bubbles.
At the surface, the turtle's head
tilts upward as it draws air into
its mouth.

Another hallmark of turtle form is their beak. Turtles have long ago abandoned the use of teeth for biting. Their toothless jaws accomplish the everyday tasks of seizing, snipping, or crushing thanks to horny beak-like sheaths lining both their upper and lower jaws. These jaw coverings, called rhamphothecae (plural of rhamphotheca) vary among turtle species and their eating habits. In vegetarian turtles like the green turtle, cutting edges of the beak are serrated into 'pseudo teeth'.

Life at Sea

Although the marine environment has allowed sea turtles to keep many of their ancestral turtle traits, some highly specialized changes to this fundamental form have been required to live a life at sea. Movement through a fluid medium demands tradeoffs. To move efficiently through water, sea turtles have had to give up some of the protections offered by their ancestral shell in return for hydrodynamic efficiency. For instance, streamlining their bodies has meant forgoing the shell-space for their head and forelimbs. Pockets beneath an overhanging shell that would accommodate these extremities would create expensive drag and reduce swimming speed. So, what would have been hollows at the neck and shoulders of sea turtles are instead bulging with the powerful muscles that drive their swimming strokes. Their shoulders are a rounded prow covered by tight but supple, almost scaleless skin that blunts the turtle's leading edge between carapace and plastron. Sea turtles can withdraw their necks into their shells, but their heads remain exposed. As a remedy to this potential vulnerability to large-jawed predators, the sea turtles have evolved robust skulls that are completely roofed over with dense bone to form a cranium every bit as tough as the turtle's shell.

In comparison to their helmet-shaped relatives, sea turtles have shells that are far more resistant to aquatic drag. The shells of marine turtles are generally a flattened teardrop shape, with roundness and posterior tapering that vary between species. In the hard-shelled sea turtles, the shell is covered with scutes that are smooth, except in juveniles of some species. In leatherbacks, the demand for a smooth hydrodynamic form has been met with a highly tapered shell covered by tight, scaleless, rubbery skin.

Certainly, the most conspicuous characters separating the sea

This hawksbill shows its tapered hydrodynamic shape.

turtles from their kin are their flippers. Sea turtle flippers are highly modified limbs used for a number of tasks, but the principal force that has driven their form is clearly the need for undersea flight. Like flight in air, fluid propulsion and control in water requires both power and steerage. For power, sea turtles use their front flippers. These are decidedly wing-like, although narrower than a bird's wing (except the penguin's wing, which they greatly resemble), and are tapered toward the tip. The front flippers are stroking hydrofoils, with leading edges blunt and trailing edges sharp, especially near the tip, where sharp scales can easily slice through human skin. Although there is a chance that razor-edged fore-flippers may have deterred a predator or two interested in eating some subsequently successful sea turtle ancestor, the greatest advantage to come from this trait is probably sheer high-performance hydrodynamics.

Inside a sea turtle's front flipper lie the standard limb bones that most vertebrates share, but with important modifications. The upper arm bone (humerus) is stubby and short, and only

When chased, a green turtle can swim at 15 mph (24 kph)

about twice as long as it is wide. About midway down the bone, a lumpy process multiplies the area of bone that the strong pectoral muscles can cling to, which allows more swimming muscle to deliver more powerful strokes. At the end of the stocky upper arm extends an even shorter set of forearm bones – the radius and ulna. These bones are fused together by fibrous connective tissue. This same tough connective tissue binds the wrist and hand bones (carpals, metacarpals, and phalanges). The widest part of the flipper blade bears the wrist and palm, with the fingers (five of them, just like us) extending outward within the

tough webbing. In the hard-shelled sea turtles, the turtle's thumb ends in a claw that pokes out at the flipper's leading edge.

As well as being wing-like in form, a sea turtle's fore-flippers are wing-like in their use. Flippers and wings trace the same motion to drive their user's flight. When viewed from the side, the tip of a sea turtle's fore-flipper can be seen to travel through an elongate figure-eight pattern. Because a turtle brings its flippers both forward and upward before stroking back and down, the figure the tip traces actually leans forward halfway between an eight and an infinity. Just as in birds, most of the power is on the down stroke.

The rear flippers of a sea turtle are just as broad and flat as the front flippers but are about half the length and are rounded at the end. The broadest part of a turtle's rear flipper is almost at the end, suggesting a shape that is less like a wing and more like the rudder of a sailing vessel. As this rudder-like form suggests, steering is exactly what a sea turtle's rear flippers do best. Following a swimming sea turtle, one can see the rear flippers perform their guiding movements. Along a straight course, hind-flippers trail "soles" down, but during turns, the inside flipper reaches out to catch the water and force the turn in its direction. In rapidly swimming turtles, the rear flippers are constantly making subtle movements to fine-tune the course.

Similar to the fore-flippers, the hind flippers are a webbed, hand-like extremity bound within a flat blade. But by comparison, the rear flippers have phalanges (toes) that are far more dexterous. The critical nature of this toe movement becomes evident as a nesting female turtle digs the neatly shaped hole for her eggs. There will be more on this amazing feat (and these amazing feet) later.

There is more to ocean life than swimming. To survive in an ocean world, sea turtles have had to adapt to many physiological challenges, not the least of which is breathing. Sea turtles take their oxygen from the atmosphere just as land animals do. Although this ties them to the ocean's surface, sea turtles do their best to push the limits of these ties during their dives. Adult turtles commonly spend 20 minutes to an hour underwater during relaxed dives, and a calm turtle in cool water may spend as much as five hours submerged. In more active dives, depths reached by turtles extend to 330 ft (100 m) or more, and in the case of the leatherback, a dive may be well over 3300 ft (1000 m) deep.

Given that sea turtles spend only about 3 per cent of their time at the surface, they are almost always holding their breath. Thus, taking along enough oxygen to survive underwater is an everyday challenge for sea turtles. But it is not enough to merely survive each dive. To survive a lifetime, sea turtles must perform underwater as they find their food and escape from their predators. Sea turtles meet these underwater challenges by having a specialized strategy for breathing, an adjustable metabolism, a tolerance for low oxygen, and an uncanny ability to squeeze more oxygen from every breath than almost any other animal.

The study of sea turtle diving behavior and physiology has benefited greatly from the design of instruments that turtles take with them into the depths and that act as vicarious observers for us. As a researcher at Hubbs Sea World Research Institute, Scott Eckert has made many vicarious observations of turtles by attaching and recovering time-depth recorders. To link the resulting dive profiles to a turtle's physiological state requires additional detective work, such as the careful descriptions of anatomy and blood chemistry from researchers at the New England Aquarium and Florida Atlantic University. From such a variety of sources, sea turtle diving is beginning to be understood in pieces so that an entire portrait of a dive can be imagined. What could it possibly be like to meet the ocean challenges that sea turtles face? What might it be like to accompany a sea turtle, such as the prodigious leatherback, during its dive? Try and imagine the following description.

Our companion leatherback is just approaching the surface on return from a modest dive of 330 ft (100 m) or so. As her head

Sea turtles are nearly always holding their breath.

breaks through the surface she is surrounded by rolling billows of exhaled air. Immediately following the forceful exhale, her head is raised to draw her next breath. Air rushes in through jaws cracked so slightly that her mouth might not even be considered open, yet the breath is made conspicuous by her bulging muscular throat. As her throat contracts, it forces a final volume of atmosphere into her lungs, and our leatherback lowers her head into a dive.

With slow strokes from her broad flippers, she glides downward toward indigo, and eventually, beyond the dimmest flicker of penetrating sunbeams. Already, her metabolism and heart rate have descended as well. With a surface resting heart rate that is already low, perhaps 20 beats per minute, our turtle's heart slows to less than one beat per minute, a rate that corresponds to a miserly use of her stored oxygen.

Continuing down beneath twilight depths, the surrounding water pressure compresses our turtle's air-filled lungs. At the surface, an average leatherback has the lung volume of a 2-liter beverage bottle, but at 1600 ft (500 m) down this volume is reduced to less than a squash ball. Rather than battle against the many tons of hydraulic force, sea turtles submit to it by allowing their lungs to collapse. With this lung collapse comes a controlled crushing of their bodies that is aided by the flexible cartilage interconnecting their bony undershell. In leatherbacks, these plastral bones are merely a girdle-like ring. Instead of the thick carapace bones seen in other sea turtles, a leatherback's shell is surrounded by a flexible mosaic of tiny bones. As the turtle continues downward, her plastron sinks in as her shell accommodates to the intense sea pressure.

Now of course, something draws the turtle to dive so deep, and this goal is food; perhaps a smack (group) of mesopelagic jellyfish, ready to be slurped down. So as if just reaching this depth were not challenging enough, our leatherback has work to do upon her arrival. It may be that we will never know how calmly a leatherback cruises at depth, searches for the faintest glimmer of potential food, and seizes its sluggishly undulating and slippery prey from the stunningly cold darkness; but we can speculate that our turtle would do all of this with a bare minimum of spent energy. She has to. After all, with a heart beat and metabolic rate only slightly higher than death, and with minimal blood flow shunted from her extremities to her brain and vital organs, vigorous activity is not only imprudent, it's impossible.

Near the end of our turtle's dive, little oxygen remains in her lungs and more of this precious gas is drawn from dissolved stores in the turtle's blood and other tissues. Leatherbacks' capacity to store oxygen in tissues outside their lungs exceeds that of the other sea turtles, and they are similar in this regard to the deepest-diving marine mammals. With diminishing oxygen also come increasing levels of toxic carbon dioxide and lactic acid, a dilemma that sea turtles seem to address with sheer tolerance. Some sea turtles have remarkable abilities to withstand high lactic acid and lack of oxygen (anoxia). It is a talent that apparently allows hibernating sea turtles in cool water to remain submerged for days, weeks, or even months.

Sensing it's time to revisit the atmosphere, our leatherback serenely directs herself toward the surface with slow, deliberate front-flipper strokes. After several minutes, the blue surrounding her lightens. As bubbles and head emerge together, a restoring breath is taken, perhaps several of them. At the end of the most strenuous dives, a turtle might need multiple, spaced breaths to purge her lungs of carbon dioxide and re-saturate her tissues with oxygen. In terms used by submariners, this surface time is equivalent to charging her batteries for the next deep dive.

Aside from breathing, one of the greatest challenges to sea turtles and other marine animals is procuring usable water. As Coleridge's Ancient Mariner observed ('...Water, water, everywhere, nor any drop to drink'), the sea does not easily relinquish its water. With about 3.5 per cent of seawater being salt (of which 80 per cent, or four fifths, is table salt, sodium chloride), extracting enough water to live on becomes a tricky and somewhat expensive endeavor.

Sea turtles are in general no saltier on the inside than most other vertebrates. To stay this way, they must actively deal with a constant invasion of toxic salts from the sea they swim in. Their method to acquire water and cope with salt is to become their own desalinization plant. As such, sea turtles incessantly purge their bodies of salt with specialized lachrymal (tear) glands behind each

Like fish, sea turtles must extract usable water from the salty sea.
Sea turtles do this by excreting excess salts within a super-saline fluid produced
by glands near their eyes. They cry themselves free of salt.

This green turtle's nose is used to smell both underwater and in the air.

of their eyes. The critical function and difficult job that these salt glands must perform is indicated by their size, which is several times the size of the turtle's brain (only the size of a plump grape in adults of most species). Although the salt glands are continually excreting a viscous fluid twice as salty as seawater, their action is most readily apparent when nesting sea turtles come to land. On nesting beaches, the thick streams of mucous from a turtle's eyes are made conspicuous by their dangling collection of sand. Of course, the tears have nothing to do with the turtle's emotional state, yet the apparent 'crying' of mother turtles has always generated great empathy from their human observers.

In feeding, sea turtles make attempts to limit the amount of seawater they take in – not an easy task when swallowing large, irregularly shaped, or slippery critters. To cope, sea turtles have a muscular esophagus that is almost entirely lined with backward-pointing spikes. These cone-like papillae are stiff with keratin. They seize hold of any item in the turtle's throat while strong throat muscles squeeze out inadvertently swallowed seawater. The papillae are especially helpful to leatherbacks who make a living packing in and keeping down bushels of slippery pulsating jellyfish.

Sea Turtle Senses

No doubt, sea turtles see, hear, smell, taste, and feel a world that is different from ours. This is largely because of the sensory filter they live in – the ocean. But a sea turtle's ability to detect and process its world is shaped not only by the challenges that the sea presents but also by its opportunities. For instance, the opportunity for extensive migrations across boundless oceans seems to have brought about an uncommon ability in sea turtles to sense where they are and where they are going. Although it is unclear which senses are most important for a sea turtle's heightened sense of place, it is likely that they use many of the senses that also serve them well in the more mundane tasks of finding food and avoiding danger.

Vision is probably one of the most important senses a sea turtle has. Just as we do, sea turtles coordinate a wide variety of important tasks based on what they see. Judging from the nature of their eye, sea turtles see well underwater but are myopic in air. More than likely, they can discriminate between colors well, although the colors they see are a bit different from the rainbow familiar to us. All of the species studied have shown an ability to

Vision is one of the most important senses for a sea turtle.

see well in the ultraviolet region of the spectrum but poorly in the red end of the spectrum. Their shift in spectral sensitivity is toward the shorter wavelengths (violets, blues, and greens) in our own visible spectrum. Not surprisingly, it is this short-wavelength light that penetrates seawater the deepest, coloring the blue world that sea turtles see for most of their lives.

To a casual observer sea turtles do not have ears and they might not be expected to hear very well. But a closer study of their anatomy reveals an auditory sense that is not only adapted to ocean life but also capable of remarkable detection. Although a sea turtle's ear is inside its head, it employs the same system for sound collection, conduction, and analysis performed by the outer, middle, and inner ears of many other vertebrates.

The part of a sea turtle's ear that collects sound is a trumpet-shaped structure made of fatty tissue. These fatty trumpets lie with their bells pointing outward just beneath the scaly skin on each side of the turtle's head. Because the density of the fatty tissue is the same as seawater, sounds from the ocean become funneled to the narrow end of the trumpet bell. The narrow end of the bell connects to a long, thin, middle ear bone called the columella (also known as the stapes). The narrow bone, which is about a third of the width of the turtle's head, conducts vibration to the cochlea of the inner ear. This inner ear also determines a turtle's sense of balance, just as it does for humans and other land vertebrates. Although hearing is probably sensitive in sea turtles, it is restricted to a range of low bass at the bottom of our own hearing scale and below – the infrasound. These are the sounds that dominate the symphony of the seas – sounds of waves pounding shorelines, of whale bellows, and of the drumming of fishes. Thus far, any sound a sea turtle might make to contribute to this orchestration has not been found.

Being covered by keratinized skin and a protective shell, one would not expect that a sensitive touch would be important to sea turtles. Perhaps it is the least developed of their senses, but sea turtles do respond to tactile feel. I have seen turtles show both exaggerated flinches at the slightest touch, and no response at all to the cutting of a skin biopsy (an experience I know to be at least a little painful). Although it is likely that the softer exposed areas of sea turtle's skin are the most sensitive to touch, they have at least some ability to detect contact even through their carapace.

It is a neat trick for an air-breathing animal like a turtle to use its nose underwater, but they do. Sea turtles have senses of both taste and smell, although of these, their ability to smell is most extensively developed. Openings to a turtle's nose are both external, above the apex of its beak, and internal, in the palate at the roof of its mouth. This allows a turtle to run either water or air through its nose in either direction. Behavioral experiments have shown that sea turtles can readily detect smells underwater. Whereas it certainly makes sense that such ability would help a turtle locate its food, the ability to detect faint odors also has long been hypothesized to allow sea turtles to orient and navigate by chemical cues.

A mysterious nasal offshoot called the Jacobson's organ adds to speculation about the nose's role in a sea turtle finding its way. This structure's wiring of nerves is different from the connections made by the main nasal membranes thought to detect smells. But both kinds of structures are connected to an olfactory bulb (the part of the brain important for smelling) that is quite large compared to other vertebrates. Some have proposed that the Jacobson's organ may involve the most intriguing of sea turtle senses, their feel for the Earth's magnetic field.

Although many animals have been shown to have a magnetic sense, sea turtles are one of few animal groups for which a highly developed geomagnetic skill has been so thoroughly described. It is a skill that involves more than a simple compass sense. But, like a compass, this ability allows a constant orientation relative to the Earth's magnetic field. Suspect players in a turtle's magnetic sense are tiny particles of an iron oxide known as magnetite. These particles, which are suspected to lie near a sea turtle's nose, might act as miniature compass needles whose orientations stimulate the turtle's brain with a sense of magnetic location. The amazing magnetic sense of sea turtles is explored further in the chapter on World Voyagers describing sea turtle migrations.

A sea turtle's awareness of magnetic fields is the sense least familiar to humans. Waters that to us appear featureless, are posted with a wealth of magnetic information for a traveling sea turtle.

Life Cycle and Life History

A convenient place to begin contemplating the life cycle of sea turtles is at the nest. All sea turtles leave the ocean to lay their eggs in nests made on sandy ocean beaches. In these nests, turtles leave behind a lot of eggs, more eggs than other reptiles or birds normally lay. In a single installment of eggs (a clutch), a female flatback may average 50 eggs in her nest, whereas a nesting hawksbill of about the same size will commonly lay 140. But a sea turtle's egg-laying work for the season is not finished with a single nest. Ridley sea turtles generally leave two to three 100-egg clutches in installments separated by roughly three weeks. By comparison, leatherbacks may lay ten or more clutches, with about 80 eggs each, separated by 10-day intervals.

All those eggs in each of those nests incubate on their own, with no attention or protection from their mother. She is occupied with the job of adding yolk and shells to her next clutch of eggs, or she might already be on her way back to her home foraging waters. For a mass of sea turtle eggs, their world during the next several weeks of incubation is a hole in the sand. They lie under 2 ft (0.5m) or so, and are hopefully above the reach of wave-wash erosion.

Each egg begins as a ping-pong-ball-sized packet of nutriment sealed within a white, parchment-like carbonate eggshell. As the female lays them, eggs are anointed with glistening, clear, lubricating fluid exuded from the cloaca. The flexible eggs leave their mother with a small dimple, like miniature semi-flat soccer balls. As such, they greet their nest and nest mates with a cushioned bounce. After a few days, the dimple in each egg is pushed out with the absorption of water from the humid nest and the eggs become turgid spheres.

The tiny developing turtles have almost everything they need within their papery eggshell. A rich yolk and watery albumen supply energy and moisture for growth, and a membranous sac (the allantios) serves as a repository for waste. The membranes and eggshell surrounding the embryonic turtle are porous, allowing the egg to breathe. Although sea turtle eggs can be momentarily inundated by the tide without harm, extended periods underwater can drown them.

A couple of weeks into incubation, an embryonic sea turtle reaches a period during which a critical determination is made – whether it will be male or female. In sea turtles, eggs incubating under cool conditions (less than 29° C or so) become male hatchlings and eggs experiencing warmer conditions become females. It remains an exasperating mystery to us just why sea turtles (and some other turtles and crocodiles) would trust their progeny's gender to environmental fate this way. In almost all other vertebrates, sex is determined by a genetically orchestrated cascade of developmental events that start the moment of fertilization. With this typical draw of the genetic cards determining gender, sex ratios of most animals tend to be roughly one male for every female. But for sea turtles, the cards determining either male or female hatchlings are arranged by nest temperature. Commonly, this results in having an entire clutch produce only one sex.

Near the end of incubation, sea turtle embryos within the egg are in a fetal curl, hunched over their remaining yolk sac. In this posture, hatchlings are bent forward on a creased plastron with their front flippers pressed to their backs. By this point, their eggshells have thinned to the point of being a chalk-flaked balloon.

This juvenile hawksbill bears no external clue revealing its sex, which was determined by the temperature it experienced within a nest of eggs incubating on a sandy beach. Warm sands make sea turtles into females, and cooler sands produce males.

Like this Kemp's ridley hatchling (left), newly hatched sea turtles escape their papery eggshell by cutting through it with a triangular point at the tip of their beak. This hatchling was left behind by its dozens of siblings and dug up from the bottom of a nest. Eggshells are normally left below the sand by emerging hatchlings.

These green turtle hatchlings (right) sense the world outside their nest for the first time as they struggle from the sand. The group emergence of hatchlings from a nest usually occurs during the cool of the evening.

Turgid with fluid, the eggshells mildly erupt as they are pierced and torn by each hatchling's egg-tooth. This caruncle (not a real tooth) is a triangular extension below the turtle's nose that slices through the eggshell as the turtle swings its head in a circle.

Over a day or two, nearly all of the successful eggs will pip, producing walnut-sized hatchlings. With the loss of fluid from the pipped eggs, an airspace is created within the nest that allows the little turtles working room for the task ahead of them. Within this pocket, hatchlings gradually envelop their remaining yolk sacs, straighten their shells, and begin to organize in convulsive group-bouts of thrashing. The unified spasms of dozens of sets of tiny flippers eventually whittle away at the sandy ceiling and elevate the mass of hatchlings to just below the surface of the beach. There they wait in quiescence for the surface sand temperature to lower, a cue they rely on to indicate nightfall. After dusk, the uppermost hatchlings begin to stir. This motion creates a top-down transfer of excitement, and in a matter of minutes a boiling mass of squirming turtles begins bursting from their nest.

At this point, all sea turtles are confronted with the first of many challenges in finding their way. Having never experienced the ocean, hatchlings must identify it, scramble toward it, and enter the relative safety of its waves as quickly as they can. Failing in this challenge means feeding a predator, exhausting limited energy, or dehydrating in the morning sun. How hatchlings make this important orientation decision is discussed in the chapter on World Voyagers.

In their sprightly run down the beach, sea turtle hatchlings begin a period of frantic activity called the hatchling frenzy. The duration of the frenzy varies between species but it commonly lasts about 24 hours. In this time hatchlings scamper from the nest, enter the wave wash, dive beneath the tumbling breakers, and beat their flippers out to sea. The incessant activity of swimming hatchlings ensures that they move quickly through the

shallow waters off the beach, waters that are commonly dense with predatory fishes that could easily suck down a little turtle.

Away from land most young sea turtles disperse into ocean currents that carry them along watery circuits that cross entire sea basins. This begins the oceanic stage of a sea turtle's life and it can vary in length from a year to a decade or more, depending on the species. In the flatback, this period in the open ocean is very short, or perhaps even nonexistent. Conversely, leatherback turtles never really end their deep-water, open-ocean phase and are likely to spend the majority of their lives far from land.

The life of young turtles in the open sea seems to be one of floating and waiting. Although a turtle may actively swim and dive on occasion, too much of this activity wastes energy that could be put into growth. It could be that a young turtle seldom really needs to exert itself to find its food. Young oceanic sea turtles live at the surface within convergence zones that collect both turtles and floating turtle habitat. Within these swirls of currents that young turtles ride, wind and water can be expected to eventually drag a variety of bite-sized, surface organisms by the nose of a quietly floating patient spectator.

For sea turtles, growth leads to safety. Risk of death decreases dramatically as developing turtles graduate from a hatchling, to stages of small juvenile, large juvenile, and adult. Population biologists estimate that only about 1 in 1000 eggs eventually matures into an adult sea turtle, and it is mostly the eggs and smallest turtles that fail in this progression. Eggs are vulnerable to land predators and erosion, and small turtles are a snack-sized swallow for many fish predators. But by the time young oceanic turtles have grown into the size of rugby balls, few predators but the largest sharks could likely make a meal of them. Up to this size, juveniles employ a number of strategies to avoid being eaten, which range from active diving to mimicking inanimate floating objects. In addition to having a shell that hardens with growth, the

Gulls are quick to snack on little turtles that misinterpret temperature cues and emerge from nests during daylight.

Sea turtle hatchlings run frantically to the sea to avoid predators and exposure to the sun. Night and early morning emergence from the nest helps them slip by predators and avoid overheating.

smallest open-sea juveniles of loggerheads, ridleys, and hawksbills add some structural defenses to deter predation. As they grow out of the hatchling stage, they develop thick shell scutes that form ridged keels of rear-pointing, spine-like projections.

For Kemp's ridleys, hawksbills, and green turtles, achieving rugby-ball size is the milestone for abandoning the open ocean and settling into shallower coastal waters. Similar-sized flatbacks have probably never left this coastal habitat. In olive ridleys and loggerheads, even large juveniles and adults may forage in the open ocean, although most loggerheads are found over shallow seabottom by the time they are half grown. All sea turtles may shift between development habitats and are unlikely to reach adulthood in the same waters they foraged as a juvenile.

The span to sea turtle adulthood rivals almost any animal, including us. Although the ridleys may reach maturity in just a little over a decade, loggerheads and green turtles do not begin to reproduce as adults for three to five decades. Longevity beyond first reproduction is a mystery, especially because sea turtles stop growing beyond adulthood. In this aspect sea turtles are like we are, with any given group of adults containing many sizes of individuals, and each size group containing a full spread of ages. Thus, in turtles and in people, the largest adult and the smallest may be no different in age.

With a cessation of sea turtle growth, there are no known marks – like the annual rings within tree trunks – that would record the passage of time in an adult turtle. Although biologists have observed the same individual loggerheads, hawksbills and green turtles on nesting beaches for 20 years or more, the limited persistence of identification tags may make this a vast underestimate of reproductive lifespan. By the same token, the loggerheads known from aquaria have been limited in longevity by the age of the buildings that house them; some of these turtles are at least 80 years old. When it comes to observations of sea turtle lifespan, it seems clear that we haven't been watching

long enough. With persistence, we are likely to find that sea turtles are among the longest-living animals on Earth.

The fortunate few turtles that reach maturity are of great value to their population. In order to make their arduous developmental journey and patience count, they will need to produce thousands of fit offspring over decades of reproductive life. For a female sea turtle, this challenge begins with a voyage over hundreds or

As this leatherback swims away from its natal beach, it may be memorizing features that will guide it back to nest as an adult.

thousands of miles to a beach she experienced only once, as a hatchling, decades ago and at one ten-thousandth her size. This return of a sea turtle to her natal beach has been long speculated but it has been demonstrated only recently. Early on in our studies of sea turtles we reasoned that it is a difficult task for a female to find a beach where her offspring will survive. Any randomly chosen coast might be too hot, too cold, too wet, too dry, too rocky, plagued with predators, or away from ocean currents that would disperse her hatchlings. So then, what better testament to a beach's suitability than one's own survival?

An empirical demonstration of returning to their natal beach existed only in the example of Kemp's ridley. For the most part, this is a turtle that nests on only one beach, a sandy stretch of Mexican coast on the westernmost Gulf of Mexico. So it was clear that at least these turtles returned to nest on their natal beach. But for other species, biologists waited for advances in genetic identification to provide definitive evidence. In 1990, this evidence came from studies in which beach-by-beach comparisons were made of green turtle DNA inherited only from the turtle's mother. These found that female green turtles sharing a nesting beach also shared the same maternal inheritance. It was clear that their mothers, their mothers' mothers, and their vast maternal lineage, had remained faithful to the same stretch of coastline for thousands of years. How sea turtles go about locating and recognizing the beach they left as a hatchling is a mystery which is discussed later.

A female sea turtle encounters her potential mates in courtship areas directly off the nesting beach, or on the long migration to her natal beach from distant foraging waters. Male sea turtles are not as choosy as females. In fact, male sea turtles have shown many notable examples of their rash mate choices, ranging from mounts of plywood models to amorous attachment to hapless scuba divers. Although females do seem to have some options for refusal, in courtship areas with high numbers of males, females may seek refuge in shallow water to avoid unwanted advances.

When coupling occurs, males are not likely to soon let go. To help them hang on, they develop a soft lower shell that snugly fits above the rear half of the female's carapace. Their thumb claws have become larger and more recurved with adulthood, allowing them to attach at points above the female's shoulders. The male's tail is long, muscular, and prehensile, which allows it to latch onto the female from behind. Males are along for the ride at the whim of the female, which includes opportunities for breathing at the surface. The attachment of a male to his mate may last several hours. This male obstinacy is not a requirement for insemination itself, but it does allow a male to guard a female that might otherwise encounter another mate. Such a subsequent encounter would dilute the original male's contribution to his offspring. This mate-guarding does not always work completely; multiple paternity does occur and clutches of eggs may have several fathers.

Males come and go during the earliest part of the nesting season, leaving females to their task of nesting. Because females store the sperm that will fertilize all their successive clutches for the season, males may find it fruitless to continue hounding already mated females later into the season. Around the world and between the species, nesting seasons vary. Outside the tropics, nesting takes place predominantly during the late spring and summer. Closer to the equator, nesting seasons expand so that almost any month may see nesting, although wet seasons seem to be favored over dry seasons, and warm-humid monsoons are favored over cooler dryer monsoons.

Throughout a four-month or greater nesting season, female sea turtles exhaust and deplete themselves for the next generation. Having crossed seas without feeding to arrive at her home beach, a female will drag herself onto land to make repeated nests into which she'll bury hundreds of eggs. In most species, the eggs left to incubate in multiple nests spend more than 15 per cent of an individual female's body mass. Only rarely are there opportunities to feed near the nesting beach. Many females may not restock their energy stores until the end of the long migration back to their foraging waters. Not surprisingly, few sea turtles are able to make this reproductive commitment every year. In most species, females replenish themselves for one to several years between these intense reproductive efforts.

A male green turtle clings to his mate using his thumb claws, rear flippers, and strong, prehensile tail.

From Sea to Land to Sea

Sea turtles do not attend to their developing young but they do what they can to ensure the most favorable conditions for their progeny's survival on land. In this effort, sea turtles rely on the positioning and construction of a sand nest made most often under cover of darkness. How a turtle leaves the ocean, creates a nest, and returns to the surf has become the most well-known part of sea turtle biology.

Nesting beaches chosen by sea turtles are almost always sandy shores exposed to the pounding of ocean waves. Gravel or cobble beaches won't do, nor will silted or muddy flats lining sheltered waters. Many sea turtles nest on oceanic island beaches or barrier strands as well as on continental shores. To know the world's sea turtle nesting beaches is to tour some of Earth's most remarkable places.

Tortuguero, Caribbean Costa Rica: Green turtles, leatherbacks, and hawksbills all share a long, western Caribbean beach made of coarse, dark, volcanic sands backed by a low dune covered with palms, cocoplum, and invading lowland rainforest.

Ostional, Costa Rica's Pacific coast: Olive ridleys nest en masse in synchronized arribadas (arrivals) that occur on a short, coarse-grained beach spanning rock outcroppings and a river that flows into crashing breakers.

Archie Carr Refuge, Florida, USA: Loggerheads nest with green turtles and leatherbacks on a barrier island beach of broken shell and quartz sand, backed by scarped dunes tufted with sea oats.

Rancho Nuevo, Tamaulipas, northeastern Mexico: On a long, dry, powder-sand beach, Kemp's ridleys emerge in synchronized daylight arribadas on blustery days that erase all but faint signs that the beach had been visited.

Ascension Island, isolated in the central Atlantic Ocean: Diverse cove beaches tucked between rocky ledges and promontories, so different that no two are alike, host nesting green turtles that come ashore amidst the great rolling breakers of the mid-Atlantic.

The island of Zakynthos, Greece: Cocoa-brown sand beaches within the wide mouth of Laganas Bay beckon loggerhead sea turtles that nest above waves rolling in from the deep central Mediterranean.

Ras Al Hadd, Oman: Where the morning sun first shines onto the Arabian Peninsula, green turtles crowd onto sets of soft, coarse-grained beaches isolated by sheer cliff faces that were once the bottom of the ancient Tethys Ocean.

Cousin Island, the Seychelles granitic archipelago: Isolated far into the Indian Ocean, a haven for seabirds also attracts hawksbills, which nest in coarse sands of crushed, bleached coral.

Crab Island, Queensland, Australia: In the Torres Strait south of New Guinea, flatback turtles emerge with the high tide, mist tawny sands over their nests, return to the surf, and dart to evade the jaws of 16 ft (5-meter) saltwater crocodiles.

Just as sea turtle nesting beaches vary upon a common theme, so do the ways that sea turtles make their nests. After a gravid female has located the stretch of beach she left as a hatchling, her next challenge is to haul herself up onto that beach. Her mobility on land is as hampered as one might expect for a marine animal. Range in limb movement, application of muscle strength, and flipper design are all tailored for frisking through fluid. Thus, to most who witness a sea turtle's emergence and nesting, the event seems to be a struggle.

The nesting struggle begins as a female approaches near-shore waters shallow enough to trip waves into breakers. On some

The first of thousands of olive ridleys emerges at sunset to participate in a mass-nesting event on a Pacific beach in Costa Rica.

beaches, the turbulent energy from crashing waves must certainly be enough to tumble a turtle onto its back. But somehow, these events are rare. Beyond the tumbling breakers and into the uprush of spent waves, the mass of the Earth tugs ever harder on the egg-laden female. Her crawl up the beach is an impeded shuffle against gravity. Her belly shell bears much of her bulk. As the wrists and forearms of her rear-pointing front flippers gouge the sand, and as her rear-flipper webbing pushes the beach behind her, the turtle moves incrementally forward.

Among the sea turtles there are two basic styles of beach-crawling. The first is the typical alternating gait that many crawling animals use – left-rear combined with right-front, then right-rear combined with left-front. This is the crawling gait of most of the smaller and medium-sized sea turtles – hawksbills, loggerheads, and the two ridleys. Green turtles, being slightly larger, and leatherbacks, being largest of all, trudge through sand with a simultaneous butterfly-stroke gait. In this, green turtles and leatherbacks dig all four flippers into the sand and heave themselves forward with a synchronous push. Flatbacks crawl with a butterfly style as well but may revert to an alternating gait when climbing or descending slopes. Turtle shape, size, and gait result in a broad tractor-like track that is different enough to readily identify most species the morning after they've visited a beach.

Most nesting turtles crawl beyond the wet sand, above the reach of typical spring tides (the highest monthly tides), and even into the dune or vegetation line facing the sea. There the nesting female prepares a nest site by sweeping sand from in front of her with exaggerated fore-flipper strokes. With her hind flippers also making wide strokes and pushing sand behind her, she slides slowly forward into the pit that her strokes have formed, nestling in so that the rear of her shell tilts down within the deepest end of a slanting depression. Here again, there are subtle differences in style between the species. In both ridley turtles, the flatback, and

the hawksbill, the body pit is a shallow, quickly dug depression made as the turtle swivels with alternating flipper sweeps. In loggerheads, synchronous fore-flipper and alternating hind-flipper strokes make a pit almost as deep as the turtle's body, with prominent spoil mounds to the pit's sides and rear. Leatherbacks make short work of their body-pit digging, but because of powerful simultaneous front flipper strokes, the resulting pit often accommodates half the depth of her enormous body. The body pit made by green turtles is the most extensive of all. Green turtles use synchronous front-flipper strokes to blast out sand three to five turtle-lengths away from a pit deep enough to completely contain the nesting female. This preparatory body pit in all species probably allows turtles to judge the suitability of the site. But in addition, the pit also creates a working space where dryer surface sand is unlikely to slide into the egg chamber she'll dig and where the depth of her eggs can be more than the length of her rear flippers (her tools for the next excavation in the nesting sequence).

At the bottom of her body pit, a nesting sea turtle digs an egg chamber with her rear flippers. Here, in contrast to her occasionally awkward use of aquatic tools for terrestrial applications, the turtle's webbed limbs seem elegantly suited. The hole for her eggs begins with careful strokes alternated between flippers. In a stroke, each rear flipper performs like a hand in a webbed glove – probing downward into soft moist grains, twisting and cupping to isolate a loose ball of sand in its palm, elevating it from the hole with scarcely a crumble reentering, and quickly rotating to the side to dump and compress the extracted sand. Then, instantaneous with the halt in one flipper's work, the other snaps forward to flick its own previously dug sand over the head and sides of the turtle. The flipper then curls almost to a fist and gracefully opens upon entering the hole to dig. After several minutes and dozens of traded digging strokes, the egg chamber deepens into a vase-shaped receptacle. It is slightly wider at the

A leatherback turtle on a beach in French Guiana sweeps sand over her nest site to camouflage her eggs.

Green turtles excavate deep pits as they dig their nest and cover their eggs.
In the dry sands of Ascension Island it is especially important for female turtles to dig down
into sand moist enough to hold the shape of their egg chamber without collapsing.

bottom than at its throat, a shape that becomes honed as each rear flipper begins contouring rotations before withdrawing its scoop of sand. This digging sequence is remarkably similar among species. But the sizes of rear flippers involved can vary from 10 in (25 cm) length in ridleys to 30 in (75 cm) or more in leatherbacks.

During any of the preceding stages leading up to egg laying, a turtle may abandon her nesting attempt and return to the sea. Difficult digging conditions, wet sand, and the presence of predators (especially humans) often prompts such a retreat. But on occasion, the reasons for withdrawal seem known only to the turtle herself.

Toward the end of digging the egg chamber, several flipper strokes often fail to reach the cavity's complete depth, even as the turtle strains with her fore-flippers to tilt her hind flippers deeper into the hole. With the last stroke comes a brief relaxation. In ridleys, loggerheads, and hawksbills, the rear flippers rest astride the egg chamber, and with flatbacks, green turtles, and leatherbacks, the flippers cover the egg chamber. In leatherbacks, one flipper is left to dangle into the hole. Then the turtle's cloaca (the vent that opens halfway down her short tail) also relaxes and partially distends into the top of the egg chamber.

The first egg falls farthest, but is resilient enough not to break. In the voluminous hole of the leatherback, the first eggs dribble down the turtle's dangled flipper for a slightly softer entry into the world. Eggs continue to come from the cloaca in ones, twos, threes, and fours, with just a few releases each minute. In most species, visible contractions accompany each egg release. These spasms in loggerhead females cause the turtles' resting rear flippers to curl upward so that her arches point momentarily skyward.

At the end of egg-laying the widest part of the egg chamber is filled with glistening white eggs. To cover her eggs, the female makes slow rear-flipper sweeps that push sand within reach into the hole. Then, compression of sand above the eggs begins with kneading motions that apply either the flat web

(in green turtles, flatbacks, and leatherbacks) or the leading edge (in other species) of each rear flipper. In Kemp's and olive ridley turtles, packing sand atop the eggs also involves several bouts of rapid side-to-side dances in which the edges of the female's plastron thump the beach sand near the clutch. During a mass *arribada*, the dull thumps from nearby turtles pounding their plastrons can sound like dueling drums.

The eggs of this olive ridley have overflowed the chamber she dug for them and may be scrambled as she attempts to cover them.

With the eggs mostly buried and packed in, the nesting female begins to obliterate the evidence that might lead a predator directly to her eggs. She reaches forward with her front flippers to dig a purchase into the beach and sharply flings the gathered sand broadly behind her. In bouts of multiple, decisive, swimming strokes, she casts dual arcing pulses of sand spray over her nest site, often slapping the sides of her shell with the conviction of each flap. Following front-flipper strokes, her rear flippers sweep side to side to spread the excavated sand. A raised head and the rush of a great breath often precede a rest between each bout of sand throwing. The intermission seems forced by exhaustion but ends abruptly with the repeat of more vigorous flipper strokes heaving sand. The casting of sand by a female takes up about one third of her time on the beach. The effort generally leaves a mound of sand a bit larger than the turtle that made it. Green turtles leave deep pits and extensive mounds resulting from

A green turtle returns to the Atlantic from Ascension Island after a two-hour nesting process.

energetic strokes made while slowly creeping forward. Leatherbacks leave even larger nests owing to the great span of their flippers and to their tendency to turn and crawl several steps between periods of sand tossing.

With a short pause after her last weary stroke of sand, the nesting female lifts her head, and in a wide-eyed, myopic, over-the-shoulder scan, she searches for the ocean behind her. It is a task whose accuracy determines whether a turtle ever reaches

the sea at all. In the leatherback, to crawl is to haul the equivalent of a small car through the sand. This effort magnifies the risk of her entrapment by obstructions landward of her nest. Thus, in what may be a response to the consequences of failure, leatherbacks commonly turn a complete orientation circle before selecting the most likely seaward direction. For Ridleys and hawksbills, the crawl to the sea ends a nesting sequence lasting less than an hour. Loggerheads and flatbacks nest for a little more than an hour, green turtles take about an hour and a half, and leatherbacks are commonly on a nesting beach for more than two hours.

After crawling from her first nest of the season and into the surf, a female sea turtle will soon ovulate her next clutch of eggs. They will be fertilized with sperm stored from her previous encounters with one to several males. The time to her next nesting attempt will be 9 to 10 days if she is a leatherback, or roughly two weeks if she is one of the hard-shelled sea turtles. However, ridleys waiting for just the right conditions to signal an arribada may forestall nesting again for three or four weeks. The nesting season for most sea turtles is spent preparing for and making from one to seven nests. Exhausted by all that is required for such a reproductive effort, most turtles will not return to their nesting beach for two to four years.

In seven to ten weeks the nest site is again a center of activity as hatchlings surge upward out of the sand. For male turtles, this frenzied dash to the sea will probably be the last time they will ever experience gravity's tug on land. For the females, at least those favored by fortune and fitness, decades may pass before they again find themselves without the familiar support of buoyancy. Again at their natal beach, these females will have come full circle.

Sea turtles, like this loggerhead, orient seaward after nesting by directing themselves toward the bright open sky over water.

World Voyagers

Every good epic journey requires a return home. For sea turtles, home is a nesting beach. It is an origin that becomes the focal point for a lifetime of travels. But throughout their long lives, most sea turtles will form and dissolve allegiances to other areas as well. These patches of habitat within widely separated ranges become transitory stops on a great life voyage.

The First Big Swim

Immediately upon their entry into the world, sea turtle hatchlings must accurately locate an ocean they've never seen and begin a swim for their lives. At its beginning, a hatchling is one of dozens of siblings erupting from a nest and out from the sandy depression above their buried empty eggshells. Amidst hundreds of tiny thrashing flippers, a hatchling scrambles to a vantage point atop the weathered mound left by its mother and stops to clumsily wipe a soft fore flipper across an eye crusted with sand. Head up in a glistening stare, rotund orbs blink, and reveal to the hatchling its first scene – a starry night sky over two opposite horizons. Choosing between the two horizons is a decision that will either lead a hatchling from nest to sea or condemn the little turtle to death within a tangled dune.

Hatchlings orient to the sea by locating the center of a bright, broad, unobstructed horizon. These characters typically match the open view of the night sky over a glittering ocean. But on coastlines modified by humans where electric lighting is visible from the nesting beach, hatchlings strive to reach an artificial brightness that overpowers the subtle cues from nocturnal celestial light. So deceived, a hatchling is unlikely to ever reach the sea. On beaches lighted only by the twinkle of stars, hatchlings crawl on precise bearings toward the brightness of an ocean, acting on a biological hunch that has proven correct for ages. But on beaches lit by the glare of electric lights, an innate movement toward brightness is likely to lead entire nests of hatchlings ever further from the sea.

As a frenzied hatchling reaches the hard wet sand of the swash zone, it nears the rush of frothy water from the exhausted breakers. To a walnut-sized little turtle, the waves are mountains. Entering the rushing sheets of water often takes several attempts as each foamy collision tumbles the tiny turtles back up the beach. Hatchlings so spit forth by the ocean right themselves with wide rotations of their head, blink to reacquire their target, and continue seaward undaunted. Crawling hatchlings with the luck to enter the rush of water at the apex of its upward movement are enveloped, and shoot down the beach with the seaward slide of the returning flow.

Suspended by water, hatchlings immediately swim. A two-second head-up breath precedes a dive into rapid front-flipper powerstroking. Still among breaking waves, a hatchling will dive just before the arrival of each looming boil of turbulence. The dive takes the hatchling beneath the crash of the wave and is elegantly performed to place the little turtle in position to be pulled out with the withdrawing undertow. Dive by dive and breaker by breaker, hatchlings make their way out beyond the surf.

Most of what is known about swimming orientation in sea turtle hatchlings comes from studies of loggerheads, but it seems likely that all species share their tactics in this challenge. The challenge is to continue seaward orientation where the visual differences between landward and seaward directions become indistinguishable to a turtle poking a bean-sized head above the surface. Within and just outside the turmoil of the surf, hatchlings begin to ignore brightness cues and instead direct themselves into

Green turtle hatchlings scramble toward the brightest horizon after a nocturnal emergence from their nest.

oncoming swells. Faith in this tactic is reaffirmed by the physics of wave motion. As swells generated anywhere out to sea approach land, part of the wave is slowed by the shallows off the beach. Thus, waves approaching the beach pivot on the end first reaching the shallow water. This refracts the wave, bending it, so that its travel is steered directly toward the shore.

A hatchling's use of wave motion for orientation is a subject that

A newly hatched green turtle pauses for a breath during its furious swim out to sea.

has been studied by researchers at Florida Atlantic University and the University of North Carolina. They have found that a hatchling bobbing and stroking through the waves senses its orientation by the orbit it makes with each wave's passage. As a wave rolls by, hatchlings swimming in the seaward direction feel movement backward, then downward, then forward, then upward, within the motion of circular movement inside the wave. Thus, a hatchling surging first to one side turns on the opposite flipper until its swimming is in line with the orbits of waves marching to shore.

As they leave the waters off their natal beach, hatchlings are but specks on a wide-open sea. Their frenzy of activity on the beach has carried over to the vigor with which they swim. About 2 ft (0.5 m) under water, hatchlings stroke fore-flippers to a constant beat for 20 seconds or so, rise to the surface for a momentary head-up breath during a four-flipper dogpaddle, and dive again to cruising depth. In these incessant cycles of powerstroking and breaths, hatchlings of most species cover the length of a football field about every five minutes.

In only an hour of swimming, a hatchling is likely to find itself more than half a mile from the beach and beyond the point where the shallows turn the waves to shore. Here the swells cannot be trusted to lead a traveler out to sea. Yet, hatchlings persist in seaward movement, having calibrated a skill in navigating they may rely on for a lifetime of journeys. This remarkable skill lies in sensing the character of the Earth's magnetic field. In sea turtles, this geomagnetic aptitude rises to levels beyond simply determining a compass direction. Already in its incipient sensations of the world, a hatchling at this milestone has not only learned the magnetic feel of movement out to sea, but it has also acquired a magnetic awareness of location applicable to any of their travels from that point forward. Much of what we know today about this remarkable skill in sea turtles comes from the work of researchers at UNC Chapel Hill led by Ken Lohmann.

Only with instruments can we sense, as sea turtles do, the variety in the magnetic envelope surrounding our planet — our magnetosphere. In this field are lines curving from magnetic pole to pole, lines that are horizontal near the equator, and inclining to vertical at the southern (off the coast of Antarctica due south of Tasmania) and northern (the Canadian Arctic) ends of the planet. In a reading of the tilt of these magnetic field lines, a hatchling assesses not only which way a pole is, but also how distant it is. In addition to this sensation of direction and latitude, hatchlings also show the ability to detect varying strengths of the local magnetic field. These strengths vary over the earth along distorted

Kemp's ridley sea turtle hatchlings
released into the Gulf of Mexico
by conservation workers.

A hatchling loggerhead swims at
a frenzied pace through a calm
surf out to deep blue waters.

gradients. Although field strength is greatest at the poles, many areas of the globe have lines of equal field strength that cross the lines of equal field-line tilt. Thus, with a reference for constant direction, with an ability to sense position on a magnetic grid equivalent to latitude and longitude, and with a magnetic memory for the places they've been, a hatchling has the essential tools of a navigator at hand: a compass, a sextant (perhaps even a Global Positioning System – GPS), and a map.

Young Turtles: Pilots or Passengers?

After a day or so of constant oriented swimming, a neonate sea turtle begins to pace itself, marking the gradual end of the hatchling frenzy. Although levels of activity during and after the frenzy vary among the species studied, all settle into a period of reduced activity before their second day at sea. Of the seven species, the flatback stands out as having a frenzy only hours in duration, which does not serve to disperse their hatchlings very far. The flatback is the only sea turtle thought to forgo an open-ocean life stage. As hatchlings of the other species end their frenzied swimming, they may be well offshore and within major ocean currents.

The progression from a dispersing propagule into a developing oceanic sea turtle is best understood for the loggerhead, whose behavior may be representative of the other species, except for the flatback. Following a successful escape from land, a loggerhead hatchling's only fuel for continued swimming is the residual yolk sac it has internalized from its egg. With active swimming, this source could last only a few days, but by resting for extended periods it could last much longer. Typically at the beginning of a little loggerhead's second day at sea, the cycle of diving and powerstroking ends and the turtle continues seaward with a more relaxed surface-swimming style. In this more relaxed pattern, a turtle holds its front flippers back with their undersides pressed against the sides of the upper shell and the only movement comes from a simultaneous frog-like kick of the rear flippers. A few times

each minute, this slow steady stroking is broken by a brief head-up four-flipper dogpaddle and breath. As if slowing from a run to a walk, this conservation of energy will be essential to a little turtle who may not chance upon food for days.

Three or more days after first entering the sea, a loggerhead hatchling has reduced its activity to only a few hours of daylight rear-flipper kicking. When inactive, the little turtles bob about in a position known as a tuck. Tucked loggerheads hold their front flippers flat against their backs and overlap their tiny rear flippers to conceal their tail. Motionless, with a lump-like profile and no exposed appendages to be nibbled at, the young loggerhead does its best to avoid confrontations with curious predators. Many of the fishes likely to take a snack-sized little turtle, such as the dorado or dolphinfish (*Coryphaena hippurus*), are perpetual swimmers that are likely to overlook an unexciting bit of inanimate flotsam.

Little loggerheads insert themselves into a dynamic ocean world where opportunities for feeding are patchy. It contains a vast emptiness where rare resources are both dispersed and concentrated by winds and currents. Where and when the sea's forces move surface waters together and press flotsam into lines, there are ephemeral oceanic oases. These are briefly assembled habitats where little floating turtles and their food can meet. The small animals on which young loggerheads feed are, like the young turtles, cast adrift. Thus, in a world where too much effort could actually take a turtle farther from its prey, the only sensible way to pursue a meal is to stop and wait for it.

The good things that come to a waiting loggerhead are often wrapped within patches of a floating golden plant called *Sargassum*. One of the brown algae with berry-like floats for buoyancy, this plant circles the Atlantic and forms the basis of a diverse community of organisms, including little loggerheads. In the western Atlantic, hatchling loggerheads that have dispersed from the beaches of the southeast U.S. end up in lines of assembled *Sargassum* where the Gulf Stream current sheers by continental shelf waters. On, in, and around the leafy amber tangles of *Sargassum*, young loggerheads feed on clinging hydroids, worms, snails, tiny crustaceans, and dozens of other creatures small enough to fit into a pint-sized turtle's mouth. On a calm sea, the subtle surface effects of one current slipping beneath another keep a bountiful *Sargassum* salad bar together. But when winds chop the sea into whitecaps, a turtle's bounty can quickly disperse away into nothingness. Seemingly capitalizing on the good fortune of finding themselves amongst food, neonate loggerheads bite at any floating shred or fleck that contrasts against the backdrop of *Sargassum* and deep blue sea. It is an indiscriminate feeding style common to all young sea turtles, perhaps in anticipation of the lengthy fast that may precede their next access to the sea's abundance. But with modern consequences that are gravely unfortunate for the turtles, this haphazard feeding commonly results in small turtles acquiring deadly loads of indigestible plastic bits and tar balls. Unfortunately, bite-sized elements of human discards are ubiquitous and are concentrated with turtles as they are swept along the ocean currents.

Poking about patches of flotsam in the wide-open sea, a young sea turtle may cross an entire ocean. For a young Kemp's ridley, green turtle, or hawksbill, this ride on the currents may last one to five years. But for a juvenile loggerhead growing up on the high seas, this travel may last well over a decade. It is astounding to imagine that a loggerhead hatched on a beach in southern Japan will circle the entire north Pacific, perhaps even multiple times, long before it reaches half the age of adulthood. It is a prodigious migration spanning tens of thousands of miles during which the turtle is largely a passenger. Yet, at the appointed time when a young turtle must leave the open ocean, a pilot's skills and abilities rise to meet the challenge.

Maturing Turtles: Homebodies or Gadabouts?

How and where a young sea turtle decides to make a living in shallow coastal waters is one of the greatest mysteries to those who study sea turtle biology. It is a decision that marks a dramatic shift in lifestyle. For a small turtle bobbing at the surface of a heaving sea thousands of feet above the cold dark seabottom,

This juvenile loggerhead, near the Azores in the eastern Atlantic, is likely to have hatched on a beach in the southeastern USA.

finding food anywhere but near the surface is not an option. Yet, for most sea turtles to complete their development into adults, they must shift their feeding to organisms that thrive on the bottom of sunlit seas.

The first juvenile green turtles to arrive in shallow coastal waters are the size of dinner plates (about 12 in or 30 cm in shell length) and have just begun to feed on algal patches and seagrass. Hawksbills and ridleys also enter coastal waters as plate-sized turtles but seek a different type of food. Juvenile hawksbills settle from the open ocean onto tropical reefs where they browse on sponges tucked into vibrantly ornamented rocks and corals. Kemp's ridleys of the same stage begin their pursuit of sprightly crabs in turbid gulf and estuarine waters.

Loggerheads and olive ridleys postpone their entry into the shallows until they are roughly the size of a serving platter (20 in or 50 cm in shell length), a size that is likely to be about one third of their weight as an adult. Of these two species, loggerheads become the most closely tied to shallow waters where they search for large, slow-moving, hard-shelled animals inhabiting seabottom types ranging from mud to reef. Olive ridleys may feed on slightly smaller bottom-dwelling invertebrates but they also spend a great deal of time in deep waters far from land where they eat a wide variety of pelagic animals.

Of all the sea turtle species, the leatherback is most reluctant to forage in coastal waters. Perhaps by specializing on large gelatinous invertebrates that are frequently concentrated in the open ocean, and perhaps because they are able to descend to tremendous depths in order to access this abundance, leatherbacks can attain adult size without ever giving up their oceanic lifestyle.

Movements of foraging sea turtles seem to be linked to their dependence upon localized food resources. For instance, green turtles grazing on seagrasses spread over underwater pastures are known to maintain closely cropped plots that they return to time and again. Their fidelity to these manicured seagrass plots ensures them access to the nutritious new growth of the lengthening grass blades. So it is not surprising that green turtles may spend years within the same patch of seabottom. In experiments where juvenile green turtles were captured from their home range and released many miles away, the turtles almost invariably swam directly back to their familiar foraging plots.

The carnivorous sea turtles like hawksbills and loggerheads also seem faithful to particular areas. Occasionally, these turtles are observed repeatedly within a small corner of hard-bottom or reef that is indistinguishable from the wide spread of adjacent similar habitat occupied by its own resident turtles. These patches of familiar habitat often contain a resting area, such as a nook beneath a rocky ledge, where turtles wedge themselves to sleep at the end of each day.

In a sea turtle's tendencies for neighborhood fidelity we again find an impressive skill made possible by extraordinary senses. One important sense in neighborhood recognition is the feel for geomagnetism that turtles first used as hatchlings. In an attempt to understand the feel that a maturing turtle has for its shallow-water home, researchers took green turtles from a Florida lagoon and placed them in tanks beneath the large wire lattice of a magnetic field coil. From the coil, they could replicate magnetic fields from locations that were hundreds of miles away from the turtles' home lagoon. It was a test to determine whether the turtles have a magnetic map in their heads that would allow them to orient homeward. And apparently, they do have just such a map. The green turtles within a field mimicking the conditions of a site north of home directed their swimming southward, and vice versa. Although it is difficult to imagine such a radical displacement from home occurring in the real world, sea turtles are seemingly able to understand their magnetic surroundings enough to deal with such an abrupt relocation.

With the sort of fixation that sea turtles have for their familiar foraging grounds, one might think that most sea turtles settle into a parochial existence as reclusive homebodies, but this is not the case. One generality among most sea turtles is that their development is spanned by many migrations between successive habitats. For example, in the loggerhead sea turtles of the western Atlantic, as young 55 lb (25 kg) turtles arrive in shallow waters,

Loggerheads like this juvenile may circle entire ocean basins before growing large enough to feed in coastal waters.

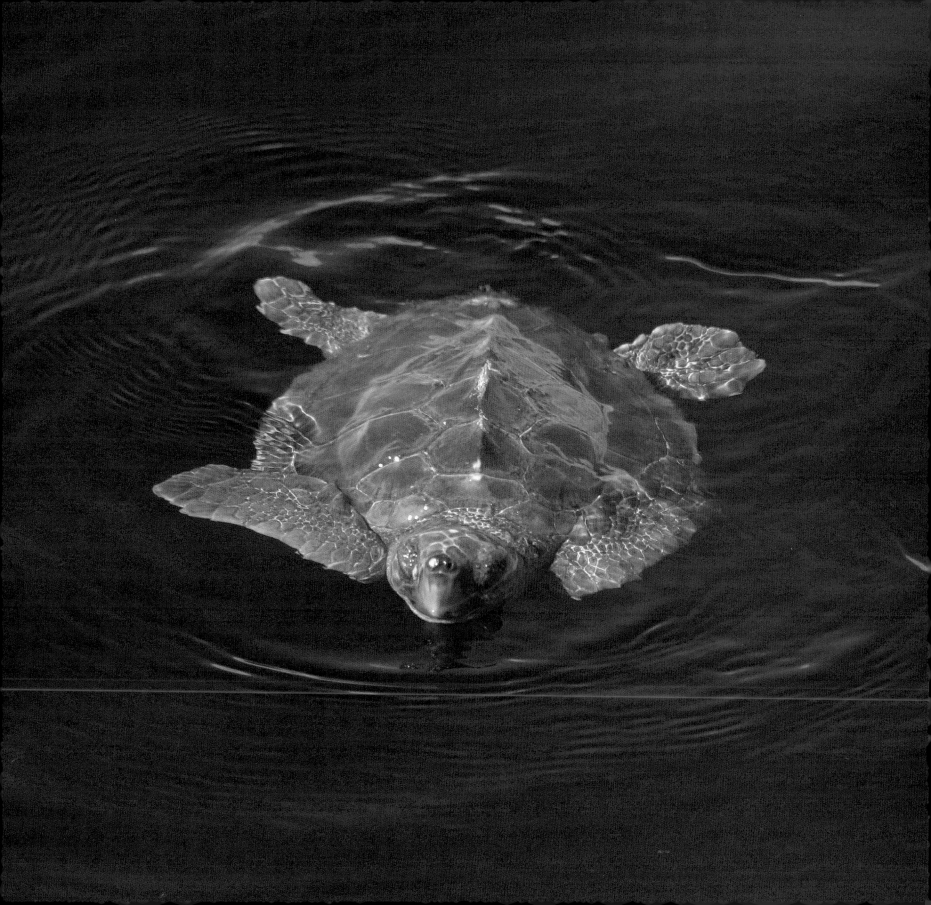

they may be found throughout the shores of North America south of New England. But as the loggerheads grow, they tend to inhabit coastal waters farther south. Upon reaching pubescence and adulthood, most loggerheads of this western Atlantic assemblage find themselves in the warm waters between the southernmost Florida peninsula, the Greater Antilles, and the Bahamas.

This gradual shift in range may be superimposed upon many seasonal migrations. Along the southeast Atlantic United States, loggerheads foraging in Chesapeake Bay and the sounds of North Carolina depart in the fall. The turtles spend colder winter months in Florida or out on the continental shelf where the warm waters of the Gulf Stream edge by. However, just as some assemblages of birds are made up of some that migrate and some that stay put, many sea turtles in tolerably warm waters find no need to swim hundreds of miles between seasons.

Among the wanderings of sea turtles, the summer-winter commutes of leatherbacks are truly global in extent. In what is the first complete glimpse of where these turtles spend their seasons, Canadian and US researchers have tracked leatherbacks with satellite-monitored transmitters. The satellite broadcasts of the turtles scatter points from their positions that trace a path from their summer range off Newfoundland to their winter range in the central Atlantic just north of the Equator. It is a yearly round trip of over 6000 miles (10,000 km). In less direct routes north to south and back again, leatherbacks from Florida nesting beaches tracked by researchers have traveled the western Gulf Stream from Florida to Nova Scotia, occasionally making extensive looping sojourns across the North Atlantic. These great loops have spanned an entire ocean basin in a season of wandering, from the Carolina's Outer Banks, to Portugal's Azores Islands, to the waters off West Africa, and to the windward fringe of the Caribbean.

Reproductive Journeys

The most impressive of grand voyages are not only extensive; they are also precise. As our own species began to set out on ocean passages, it was the precision part of the exercise that proved to be the greatest challenge. Traveling across a vast and featureless sea from point A to a distant point B required considerable problem-solving skills and technology. Most people find it astounding that a sea turtle with none of these advantages can accomplish such a challenging navigational task. It is a bewilderment that underscores how little we know about the intimate connections between sea turtles and their world.

Archie Carr, considered to be the most influential pioneer in understanding and interpreting the lives of sea turtles, continually marveled at their navigational precision. In what is still one of the most compelling descriptions of this ability, Carr traced the voyages of female green turtles that had been marked with flipper tags on the nesting beaches of the mid Atlantic island of Ascension. Over years, a picture of the voyages of Ascension green turtles slowly developed. Returns of the tags came from fishermen who had caught the turtles far to the west, 1200 miles (2000 km) or more away, in the waters off Brazil.

Ascension is easily overlooked. It is but a speck of land – a single exposed seamount in the center of the equatorial Atlantic so neatly between Africa and South America, so isolated, and so inconspicuous that the place often goes unrepresented on maps. Yet, Ascension Island serves as one of the most important nesting aggregations for green turtles in the world. Before the arrival of British sailing ships and an island garrison, a human occupancy that consumed about 1500 nesting turtles per year during a large part of the 19th century, the number of green turtles visiting the island was even greater than the 2000 to 3000 annual visits seen today.

This young green turtle in the shallow waters surrounding Borneo is small enough to have just graduated from the open-ocean stage of its life. Most sea turtle species disperse from beaches as hatchlings and remain within oceanic surface currents for one to several years.

The circuit between Ascension and Brazil involves a round trip approaching 3000 miles (5000 km) over a deep ocean basin with no opportunity for green turtles to feed. Thus, a green turtle must store in the fat reserves and developing egg follicles she takes with her, every calorie of energy required to make the arduous trip. This means surviving for three or more months, producing more than

Place memories that persist for decades help guide the lives of green turtles.

44 lb (20 kg) of eggs, burying and hiding them in four installments or so, and swimming the long return to Brazil. With this task at hand, green turtles heavy with eggs set out from their seagrass meadows and algal patches throughout Brazil's long tropical Atlantic coast to cross an ocean and locate a seemingly impossible target.

It is a job that would be difficult enough for turtles that made a regular commute to Ascension. But consider the task of a female approaching her first reproductive season. There, on her familiar pastures off the northern shelf of South America, fattened and restless, she draws upon a memory registered 30 years or more

ago when a tiny, frantic hatchling was swimming for its very life. And with whatever clarity has remained in that recollection, an experience first imbedded in a brain the size of a sesame seed, a green turtle is guided on her journey.

Through the work on sea turtle genetics done by Brian Bowen, then at the University of Florida, in conjunction with colleagues from all over the world, it now seems clear that this persistence of natal memory is key to a female green turtle returning to her home beach. Evidence for this comes from a close examination of the relatedness of green turtles that share foraging areas but migrate to different nesting beaches. The rich coastal waters at the eastern bulge of Brazil serve as foraging grounds for green turtles that nest either at Ascension, or westward on the northern coast of South America in Surinam. Although the overlap on their feeding grounds is broad, individual tagged turtles have never been seen to have more than a single nesting area. This faithfulness to a beach is also revealed in the turtle's DNA that is passed on only from mother to daughter (mitochondrial DNA). With extensive sampling of mitochondrial DNA, green turtles nesting in Surinam and those from Ascension were found by Bowen and others to have distinctly different genetic markers. The results showed that green turtles have a high degree of faithfulness to their natal beach, a trait called philopatry. It is a trait that has been shown for all the species of sea turtles examined and would seem to add eidetic memory to a sea turtle's list of useful navigational skills.

Lately, Ascension Island has become a laboratory in the study of how sea turtles can accomplish such pinpoint navigation. University of Wales researchers Brendan Godley and Graeme Hays along with Floriano Papi and Paolo Luschi at the University of Pisa have worked to challenge the senses of green turtles desiring to nest at Ascension. Challenges to turtles have included being displaced over 60 miles (100 km), either upwind or downwind from the island, and in some trials, turtles bore magnets strapped to their heads. Remarkably, even without the opportunity for an upwind sniff of their goal, and with their detection of the geomagnetic field presumably overwhelmed by the bar magnet they carried, green turtles driven to nest consistently found their way back to Ascension.

The results from this mid-ocean laboratory suggest the depth of what we don't know about the ability of sea turtles to sense and move in their world. At present, there are many sensory modalities that have been proposed as ways that sea turtles navigate. But the rigorous experiments required to demonstrate how a turtle uses its skills are difficult, and few hypotheses have been discarded. The magnetic map hypothesis is still a valid explanation of some of the biological instrumentation in the sea turtle navigator's toolbox, along with abilities to smell and measure wind waves. It seems likely that the toolbox of Ascension green turtles is well stocked. By a number of senses and types of landmarks, perhaps used within a system for both recognizing reliability and reverting to contingencies, green turtles know well their way to Ascension.

The Ascension Island example is but one of many lengthy crossings between sea turtle feeding areas and nesting beaches that biologists have observed. For instance, leatherbacks foraging in the North Atlantic off Nova Scotia voyage to nest just a few degrees from the equator in Surinam and French Guiana, a one-way trip approaching 3100 miles (5000 km). Why sea turtles travel so far to lay their eggs has been a vexing puzzle to biologists, although we do have our ideas.

One idea is that the best feeding areas and the best nesting spots seldom occur together. For instance, the Ascension Island green turtle beaches seem perfect for producing young. There are no mammalian predators to dig up eggs (at least there were none before humans arrived), and a short swim out from the island puts hatchlings directly into their oceanic habitat and away from the coastal fishes that would make a meal of them. The trouble is, Ascension is surrounded by nothing that would interest a hungry adult green turtle. Beneath the waters around the island there is a barren slide down to more than 2 miles (3km) deep, allowing little growth of the vegetation that green turtles need to grow up and make little turtles. However, the same limitations on foraging opportunities do not exist for the island nesting beaches just off Brazil's easternmost coast where hundreds of green turtles choose to nest. Intermingled off Brazil's coastal foraging grounds are not only the green turtles faithful to Brazilian beaches, but also the thousands of equally faithful green turtles whose beaches range as far west as Costa Rica and as far east as Ascension. So it seems that the perfect nesting beach may be as elusive a concept for sea turtles as it is for us.

Just as there are differences of opinion on the adequacy of nesting beaches, so are there differences concerning where the best feeding places are. On the black sand beaches of Tortuguero on Costa Rica's Caribbean coast, tens of thousands of green turtles have had the trailing edge of their front flippers tagged with numbered stainless steel clasps meant to identify the turtle should it be seen again. Hundreds have been, most often by someone who has captured the turtle to eat it. The annual tagging effort was a study of green turtle dispersal begun by Archie Carr in the late 1950s. Carr hoped that anyone who saw the turtle and noticed the tag would read the terse reward statement and return address printed on it and post a letter describing where they saw it. They did. In terms of numbers of verified connections between a nesting beach and its turtles' foraging grounds, the Tortuguero tagging project has been the most successful study of sea turtle dispersal ever conducted.

My opportunities to discuss the subject of sea turtles with Professor Carr came only in the final years of his life. I recall him as active and vibrant, and although he was not taking on graduate students, he offered a tour of his office at the University of Florida and introductions to faculty who might accept a student interested in questions about sea turtles. There in his office I first saw the map – a chart of the Caribbean studded with hundreds of green pins designating the tag-recovery locations from well over a thousand green turtles tagged at Tortuguero and seen again elsewhere. There was a dense cluster of green north of Costa Rica off the eastern tip of Nicaragua – the Miskito Cays. And there were pins farther to the north off Yucatan, Jamaica, Cuba, Hispaniola, and the Bahamas. To the south, green pins poked from waters off Panama and Colombia, and eastward to Venezuela. In one sense, the map was a grim statement of how broadly the taste for green turtle affected the population whose reproduction centered on Tortuguero. In another sense, it showed how widespread the population was, even though their breeding focused on only a tiny strip of Costa Rica shoreline. It may be that maps like this also represent the diasporas and pilgrimages of lesser-known sea turtle populations as well.

Of all the sea turtles, hawksbills may make some of the shortest commutes between feeding areas and nesting beaches. But many of these trips are likely to take turtles over open waters between islands, and from one country's waters to another. Rare is the sea turtle of any species that lives out its life in the seas of a single nation. Thus, the migrations of sea turtles make them both multinational and international travelers, linking them as a resource to human communities spread throughout the globe.

Navigational Talents of Animal Savants

Most of us would never strike out on our own to travel the world without the technological trappings designed and built by legions of brilliant scientists and engineers. Without technology, we are lost. It makes us realize what a tricky business navigation is. Without our satellite receivers, maps, compasses, and clocks, we are naked and, when it comes to navigating, a bit stupid.

The ability of sea turtles to travel the globe and return precisely to specific locations astounds us. This is partly because we admire the talent, much in the way that we admire the geniuses of our own species. But the special talents of sea turtles astonish us further by the humble package that contains them. After all, sea turtles are but simple reptiles, without the traits of sapience we reserve largely for ourselves. Yet, they are creatures that accomplish remarkable feats of intelligence. They seem to know where they are, and almost wherever they are taken, they are able to direct themselves to where they would like to be. They do this by using senses, memory, and calculations of direction that seem to show absolute brilliance. But in the simple intelligence tests that are often applied to animals – for instance, quickness to learn where food is by trial and error – reptiles as a group do poorly compared to larger-brained creatures.

Sea turtles are animal savants. By comparison to other animals, they may be either simple or clever. As such, they accompany a host of other brilliant simpletons, from birds to insects, which have also shown their navigational talents. However, sea turtles remain unique in their aptitude for the specific tasks that allow them to survive in their own world. Pinpoint navigation across an ocean to a dot of land may have had its origins within the simplest animals, but the expression of this skill by sea turtles seems singularly appropriate for their unique lives. At some time when we are able to fully understand the awareness that sea turtles have of their world, we will have taken great strides towards better understanding our own.

This hawksbill, at home on its neighborhood reef in the South China Sea, knows its world in a way we can only imagine.

*The sun sets on a Pacific beach in Costa Rica as an 'arribada'
begins. Before the night is over, thousands of female olive ridleys will
crowd onto this small stretch of beach to lay their eggs.*

The Role of Sea Turtles

The role that sea turtles play in running the world – their ecology – is difficult for us to comprehend. After all, sea turtles live on a grand geographic scale, which greatly limits our ability to observe and measure their effect on the equally vast ecosystems they occupy. These systems are generally more poorly known than terrestrial systems. As in most animals, the ecological place of sea turtles is determined not only by their presence but also by their abundance. So in a world where we have only shadows of historical numbers, the influence of sea turtles must be subdued. With the decline of sea turtles, many aspects of their world, and of our world, have changed.

One conspicuous example of an important remaining influence between sea turtles and their environment can be seen in profound events that occur where we terrestrial beings can easily watch, the *arribadas* of ridley turtles. In some populations of the olive ridley, these events are still prominent enough to deserve a description as grand ecological phenomena. In Spanish, the word *arribada* simply translates as 'arrival', an English term that seems to fall short in describing the event's significance.

One stage for this remarkable gathering of organisms is a short stretch of dark volcanic sand on Costa Rica's Pacific shore. Most nights out of the year, this beach near the tiny village of Ostional may see one to several olive ridleys, locally called tortuga golfina, emerging from the sea to put their eggs in the sand. But once each month during the last half of the rainy season, a ridley convention builds. Responding in unison to cues that are not well understood, olive ridley females converge by multitudes into the waters out from the line of breakers tumbling onto Ostional Beach. Some lunar influence seems present because of the monthly separation of events, although many phases of the moon may light these gatherings. Similarly, a strong wind out to sea seems to correlate with ridley arrivals, but not always. Whatever the synergy of weather, tide, and moon convincing ridleys they should nest, the argument must be compelling, for only a small fraction of ridleys choose to nest without the company of this massive building crowd.

Just before nightfall on the first night of an *arribada*, the gathered turtles begin their invasion of the beach. Like landing craft they emerge from the wave-wash and trudge up the beach. Some crawl shoulder to shoulder, some advance on others, and some rest momentarily and are nudged aside by the more anxious among the building throngs. By midnight, advancing waves of domed silhouettes completely fill the lower beach, and sights and sounds of tens of thousands of digging, huffing, sand-scattering turtles consume the upper beach. With a beach length of only 800 linear meters, every meter of Ostional's shore will be visited by more than a hundred nesting ridleys over the next two or three nights.

To a naive witness of this event, the invasion is a disaster. Turtle after turtle thrusting her hind flippers into the sand withdraws the sticky yolk from pierced eggs that were buried by the turtle she had just pushed aside. Turtles covering their nests unearth more eggs, flinging shells, and dripping egg contents upon themselves and their dozen or so diligently nesting neighbors. And to this carnage come silhouettes of cautiously curious animals drawn by the thick smell of fat-rich yolks. In the darkness, feral dogs and raccoons tunnel into partially exposed nests amidst the vastly spread pile of turtles pursuing their single-minded task.

At the lightening of the hazy sky over the jungle behind the beach, only a thousand or so ridleys remain from the tens of thousands that had visited. As they crawl down the beach to the sea, they scuff through drifts of gleaming eggshells that cover the breadth of the beach like a dusting of snow. In the creeping daylight, raccoons and dogs hustle with distended bellies through flocks of black vultures hopping and skipping as the skimmed golden riches drip from their beaks.

This visible scene of devastation overlies a less evident one. Infused in the sand are the turtle-deposited nutrients that have turned the beach from antiseptic wave-washed sand into an enormous petri dish rife with pathogens. Developing eggs that have not been penetrated by insect larvae frequently succumb to infections from the soup of bacteria and fungi in which they incubate. Of the immense load thrust upon the beach, only a small fraction of the eggs will produce hatchlings. Although the fraction of hatched eggs may be small, the great number of original eggs laid makes for a profoundly important mass departure of hatchings some two moons after the tumult of the *arribada*.

Hatchlings seem to be everywhere. Over only a few nights, one million or more tiny dark gray ridleys bubble from nests and flow down the beach to the sea. It is the event that brings fruition to the preceding *arribada*, and it is every bit as popular with the local predators. Although the nocturnal timing and surprise of this potential bounty allows most hatchlings passage by overwhelmed beach crabs and night herons, tardy hatchlings still on the beach at break of day become helpless tidbits for vultures, cara caras, coatis, and dogs.

Taking stock of effects on the slice of the world where olive ridleys have chosen to nest, we see an animal with many important relationships. On the short Ostional beach alone, nesting ridleys bring nearly 4.5 million pounds of eggs each season, much of which is converted into other organisms, including human beings. The few hundred people who live in the Ostional village gather roughly 10 per cent of the eggs laid, for consumption throughout Costa Rica. This predation is managed by the government to occur mostly at the beginning stages of each *arribada*, a strategy that is thought to ensure that mostly 'doomed' eggs are taken. Of course, also in the line of benefiting predators and scavengers are the multitudes of other mammals, birds, reptiles, fishes, crustaceans, insects, fungi, and bacteria that eat turtle eggs, or that eat the things that eat turtle eggs.

In all, the *arribada* phenomenon is a grand ecological event. Yet, the richness brought to a tiny area of sand and its adjacent waters does not explain the reason for an *arribada*. Selection for this intense reproductive gathering lies with its success in making little turtles, not with feeding the neighborhood. So, is it successful? With its persistence, we assume so. Although the mortality of eggs is high, the hatchlings that emerge do so in a massive, largely unanticipated pulse that probably overwhelms and surprises potential predators. But it is also clear that the *arribada* is not the single correct answer to the problem of maximizing reproductive success. Apparently, the solitary ridleys that nest on the beaches fringing the main *arribada* beach and during periods between mass nestings benefit from a strategy of inconspicuous 'flight beneath the radar' that rivals the bold confrontation of *arribada* turtles.

The unintentional contribution made by sea turtles to the coastal ecosystems they breed in is significant for many major nesting beaches. In their calculation of the nutrients contributed by Florida loggerheads to their nesting beaches, researchers at the University of Florida found these turtles to be major sources of nitrogen and phosphorous. In the 660,000 lb (300,000 kg) or so of eggs that loggerheads bury on Florida beaches every year, much remains as the organic residue of reproductive failure. This lingering nitrogen and phosphorous, which amounts to thousands of pounds of fertilizer each year, greatly benefits the plants that struggle to grow on the nutrient-poor dunes. In this transportation of nutrients between sea and land, sea turtles glean energy and compounds critical to life over hundreds of thousands of square miles and intensely focus their ecological delivery onto single stretches of sandy coastline.

Although the effects of sea turtles on land are easiest for us to see, their effects on marine ecosystems are certainly the most

The unhatched eggs left behind in the nests of these green turtle hatchlings are an important nutrient source for beach plants.

Hawksbills eat a particular array of sponges and fulfil a unique ecological role on coral reefs.

important. In what may be a parallel between grassy ecosystems on land and in the sea, a single species of grazing animal can be instrumental to the basic function of an ecosystem on which thousands of species depend. Green turtles certainly were, and to a lesser extent are now, influential grazers of seagrass and algal pastures.

Sea turtle ecologist Karen Bjorndal has estimated that the Caribbean basin once supported over 30 million adult green turtles. This figure is comparable to the abundance of American bison that once grazed the great tall-grass prairies of North America. Like the great herds of bison, Caribbean green turtles must have been integral to the functioning of the marine meadows they foraged in. Dr. Bjorndal and Alan Bolten have speculated that the Caribbean seagrass pastures of today, grazed by green turtles at only about 5 per cent of their historical abundance, have undergone important changes. Before North and South America were on the maps of technologically capable Europeans, the vast shallows of the greater Caribbean were crowded with green turtles, seagrass meadows surged with productivity from the continual cropping by serrated turtle beaks, and nutrients were spread widely with the cigars of dung that traced the movements of green turtles throughout their broad range. Today, many grazers of seagrasses remain, but the unique close-cropping grazing style of the green turtle is far less influential. On Caribbean seagrass pastures of today, one commonly sees long uncropped blades encrusted with surface-growing organisms. These grass blades often go ungrazed, brown with age, and detach to lock their nutrients within accumulating detritus. Much of the nutrient store held in the blades of seagrasses may be liberated only as the dead vegetation slowly rots away. Due to the decline of green turtles, an ecologically important short-circuit to the seagrass detritus cycle has begun to fail.

Sea turtles tend to be generalist feeders, with lists of food items that include many dozens of species. Even leatherbacks, with a narrow definition of what makes good food that includes only

animals with the consistency of jelly, and green turtles, who as larger turtles eat mostly vegetation, have relatively wide preferences in terms of numbers of species eaten. These catholic tastes tend to minimize effects from sea turtle predation on any one organism (with the possible exception of the green turtle's favorite greens, turtle grass, *Thalassia*), but spread the influence of sea turtles around the breadth of the ecosystems they inhabit.

Green turtles eat mostly seagrasses and algae but will feed opportunistically on animals including jellyfish.

As prey, hatchling sea turtles fit into the diet of 100 or more species of fishes and marine birds. But as sea turtles attain size, fewer and fewer predators at sea are able to eat them. One ocean predator that stands out as equipped to eat large sea turtles is the tiger shark (*Galeocerdo cuvier*). These grand fish have the gape, jaw strength, and robust tooth shape that make them a specialist in chewing large chunks off big tough animals, including sea turtles. A tiger shark's teeth have a thick broad base and a laterally directed point that creates a V-shaped serrate cutting edge. Their advantage allows the shark to easily remove limbs or extract a mouthful of bony carapace from large turtles either living or dead. Although it is not uncommon for living adult sea turtles to have a broad crescent-shaped piece missing from the edge of their shell, or to have a missing chunk of carapace correspond with a flipper amputation, predation by sharks and mortality from their attacks are by no means rampant. In sea turtles that achieve adult size, predation other than by man is probably a rarity. Many turtles that are attacked by sharks survive even after the shock and blood loss of a ragged limb amputation, an astounding feat that seems near the pinnacle of toughness in the animal world.

Relationships between sea turtles and their world extend to a variety of animals that call a turtle their home. Most species of sea turtles have at least a few tag-along species growing on them. These tag-alongs are commensals – animals and plants that gain by living on a turtle but that have little effect upon their host, either positive or negative. Loggerhead sea turtles are exceptional for their tolerance of a diverse array of clinging commensal creatures. On a single loggerhead, one might find dozens of hitchhiking species.

Perhaps it is the relative sluggishness of loggerheads relative to the other sea turtle species. Or, perhaps it is the crusty irregularity of a loggerhead's carapace, a surface not unlike the hardened benthic substrate over which they commonly feed. But whatever traits bring about their propensity to host rides, many loggerheads find themselves as a living, traveling reef. To pore over a loggerhead's encrusted carapace is to witness an entire community of normally bottom-growing organisms – barnacles of several species, long tufts of colonial hydroids, thumbnail-long amphipods with leg specializations for clinging and lashing at tiny prey that flow by the turtle, shelled mollusks of all types, marine worms, small to hand-sized crabs, sea urchins, sea cucumbers, many species of macro algae, and even stony corals.

At least one barnacle species is almost obligated to be on a sea turtle – the turtle barnacle, *Chelonibia testudinaria*. All sea turtle species are known to sport these sessile crustaceans, which are seldom found anyplace else. Whereas turtle barnacles typically grow on a turtle's shell or head and become as large as half a golf ball, other smaller species are also common. One group of barnacles has members that embed themselves in a sea turtle's skin or that thrive attached to the turtle's bulbous tongue.

It seems clear that the barnacles benefit from easier access to items of food that are either disturbed by the feeding turtle or that flow with the sheet of water over the turtle as it swims. Heavily fouled turtles, as some loggerheads can be, probably suffer some decrease in swimming speed. This added drag would probably matter most for the smallest turtles, which have yet to outgrow the mouths of potential predators. Yet, these smallest turtles are also the fastest growing, and in frequently shedding their shell scutes they may be able to keep their backs clean by periodically ridding themselves of their acquired hangers-on.

Even fish capitalize on the habitat that sea turtles have to offer. Suckerfish (remoras) may be so numerous that they drape a large turtle like a flowing cloak. Small green turtles I have seen have had suckerfish as large as themselves suctioned to their plastron. Sometimes, the presence of these fish appears a bit annoying to the turtle, who may squirm to no avail in attempts to detach its unwanted fishy appendage. But other relationships between fish and turtles seem beneficial to both parties. Hawksbills and green turtles are known to frequent predetermined stations on a reef and assume a neck-out and flipper-spread posture in order to invite visits by cleaner fishes. With the dreamy look of a cat having its chin scratched, a supplicant turtle receives attention from a crew of wrasses, gobies, or tangs, which glean algae and tiny invertebrates with precise nibbles.

Suckerfish rely on a passing leatherback for safety and feeding opportunities.

The Species

How Many Kinds of Sea Turtles are there?

There are seven species of sea turtles... or perhaps eight. It is a debate that reaffirms the uncertainty of science, and it is a controversy that adds a bit more ambiguity to an already mysterious group of animals.

When most people think about species, they think of organisms with a particular look that are grouped together because they are similar. But the concept of a species is broader and more detailed than this, and it is an integral component to understanding how living things evolve, fit into their worlds, and interact with each other.

In practice, sea turtles and most other creatures are divided into species by two general sets of criteria: how they look and how they act. The look of a sea turtle involves much about its form – ranging from highly variable traits like size and color to less variable traits like bone sutures, scale counts, and the presence or absence of unique structures. How a sea turtle acts, or has acted, applies to whether turtles from a recognized group would ever, could ever, interbreed with turtles from another recognized group and make little turtles that themselves grow up to breed. Underlying each of these concepts is the genetic makeup of a sea turtle. Genes, of course, determine how a sea turtle looks and acts, but they also reveal a turtle's history. Studying the genetics of a group of sea turtles can reveal roughly how long the group has been separated (reproductively isolated) from another sea turtle group, how great that separation is, and whether it is enough to warrant labeling the group a separate species.

The first taxonomists to begin classifying sea turtle species used common sense to guide them and did not have access to information about genetics. Thus, sea turtles that looked different were often labeled as being different. However, some species were lumped together because rare turtles were thought to be variants of more common ones. In the eighteenth and nineteenth centuries, it was difficult to determine how different a group of turtles had to be in order to be a species.

The olive ridley has an open-ocean lifestyle that differs from its cousin, Kemp's ridley.

To truly represent a group of animals well, taxonomists like to study many individuals throughout their range. Yet, many sea turtles are large animals with wide distributions. One doesn't just fill up museum drawers with dozens of sea turtles like a curator can with pinned butterflies and stuffed mouse skins. So on occasion, a great deal of inference about species was made from a single specimen, or from just a few of them coming from a narrow slice of a turtle's range.

The green turtle is a widely distributed species with much variation in adult size and appearance.

With all the obvious limitations of studying specimens throughout their range at the time of the mid eighteenth century, Carl Linnaeus (considered the father of taxonomy) recognized three sea turtle species (the only three he had opportunity to study) and lumped them into a single genus grouping along with all the other turtles. Since then, five additional species have been recognized (or

Hawksbills occasionally hybridize with loggerheads or green turtles.

discovered). It is both remarkable and reassuring that the common-sense species descriptions from limited assessments made about 150 to 250 years ago apply to many of the species commonly recognized today. However, one of the eight species recently described has retained a controversial status and is widely believed to be a set of populations with unique traits rather than a separate species. This controversial species is the east Pacific green turtle (or black turtle), *Chelonia agassizii*, a sea turtle that many maintain is just a smaller and darkly pigmented green turtle. In deference to the majority opinion that black turtles are a variation of the green turtle, more discussion of this controversy is within the green turtle account on page 70.

Sea Turtle Hybrids

Sea turtles, it seems, hybridize. Reports have described turtles captured from the wild that by all appearances, and by examination of their genetics, are offspring of green turtles and loggerheads, of green turtles and hawksbills, of loggerheads and hawksbills, and of loggerheads and Kemp's ridleys. This in itself does not break the species rules, unless these hybrids go about reproducing themselves, which apparently happens.

To completely comprehend the shock one should feel at this revelation, one needs to understand the distance separating the species of sea turtles involved in these hybrid pairings. Depending on the pairing, these hybrid offspring had mothers and fathers whose lineages have differentiated from each other over 10-75 million years of evolution. It is equivalent to the distance separating horses and dogs, mice and monkeys, or cats and rabbits. Quite possibly, sea turtles are distinguished among the vertebrates in having the most distantly related lineages capable of producing successful hybrids in nature.

Sea turtle hybrids are odd and seem to be rare. Yet, whatever disadvantages hybrids possess have not kept some from reaching adulthood. In at least one instance, probable hybrids have laid eggs on nesting beaches, and those eggs have produced living hatchlings. This does break the species rules (as if we should expect the natural world to follow our rules), but more importantly, it raises questions about whether declines in sea turtle abundance and rarity of mates may be changing the very integrity of the species we think we know.

It is not easy to place sea turtles into simple, neat, species categories.

Green Turtle

Scientific Name

Chelonia mydas.
Named for the Greek roots for turtle and for the king of Phrygia to whom Dionysus gave the power to turn all he touched to gold.

Other common names

Other English names given the green turtle include green sea turtle, greenback turtle, soup turtle, and edible turtle. The distinctive form in the eastern Pacific is known as the black turtle. In Latin America, common names include tortuga verde and tortuga blanca (Spanish). Hundreds of other common names vary among cultures.

Size and weight

Adult female green turtles weigh between 175 and 485 lb (80 and 220 kg), with a shell straight-length of 30 to 47 in (80 to 120 cm).

The largest green turtles reach 153 cm in straight shell length and 650 lb (295 kg) in weight. Adult males are slightly smaller than females.

Distribution

Tropical and warm temperate marine waters worldwide. Nesting occurs on beaches mostly in the tropics, the major nesting beaches lying within latitudes 20° north and south.

General Appearance

Green turtles are sleek, powerful swimmers that grow to the largest size of any of the hard-shelled sea turtles. Contrary to the suggestion of color in their name, green turtles do not appear very green. Their common name comes from a description of their appearance on the inside rather than on the outside. When the insides of a green turtle are brought into the light, the fatty tissues show a greenish hue. The name is testament to how green turtles first came to be known, namely, as food. In fact, the greenest thing about a green turtle is likely to be green turtle soup. The broth is rendered from the calipash, a light green, fatty, gelatinous meat lined in irregular patches inside the carapace, and calipee, a similar light yellow-green meat attached to the interior of the plastron.

On the outside, green turtles are lovely animals. Their shells are often un-fouled by barnacles or other clinging creatures, which allows the coloration of their patterned shell to be clearly visible.

Adult green turtles vary in shell coloration between populations. A typical carapace coloration is a brown or olive background blotched with lighter patches and spattered with occasional dark brown or black. Variations in this pattern include mottling of brown, yellow, olive, and gray throughout nebulous background color. In the east Pacific green turtle, the adult's carapace is dark olive, dark gray, or black. Plastron coloration in adult green turtles ranges from blotched olive gray in east Pacific turtles, to butter yellow or dark amber in most other populations.

Juvenile green turtles are often vibrantly patterned. Carapace scutes and larger scales of the head and flippers typically show streaks of brown, olive, gold, black, and reddish brown, streaks that radiate as sunbursts from the rear margin of each scale. An imperceptibly thin film of algae may make some turtles appear greenish; although the upper sides of most turtles seem brown from a distance. Juveniles have a lighter yellow plastron than adults do, and the plastrons of the smallest

Adult green turtles feed on marine plants and reach an average weight of about 350 lb (160 kg).

juveniles (from the oceanic stage) are immaculately white.

In most green turtles, the scales crowning the head and on the upper surface of the flippers match the coloration of the carapace. Outlines of the scales (the seams) are lighter than the scales themselves. These light olive or yellow scale outlines are often the same color as the skin covering the shoulders and neck, which has sparsely scattered small scales.

Hatchlings are about 2 in (5 cm) in shell length. Their coloration is dark blue-gray to black on their upper surface and pure white below. A hatchling's carapace and flippers are thinly rimmed with white, and dark centers of their lateral head scales often give an appearance of having freckled cheeks. The skin covering a hatchling's shoulders and neck ranges from olive to blue gray.

The shape of a green turtle's shell is a teardrop, flattened below, domed above, and slightly flanged at the sides. The shell's surface is smooth, with scutes that do not overlap and that are typically shed in one piece as the turtle grows. The number of carapace scutes is almost invariable in green turtles, making these counts useful in helping to separate green turtles from other sea turtle species. Green turtles have four lateral (also called costal) scutes on either side of the midline of their carapace. Their head scales are also distinctive in that there are only two elongate scales (called prefrontals) between the turtle's eyes.

Although there is noticeable variation in size, shape, and color among green turtle populations throughout their worldwide range, green turtles of the eastern Pacific seem the most different. East Pacific green turtles are considered by some biologists and many casual observers to belong to a different subspecies of green turtle, or even to a different species altogether. East Pacific green turtles are also known as black turtles, or in western Mexico where they nest, as tortuga prieta or tortuga negra.

Among the characters separating east Pacific green turtles from other green turtles around the world, the most vivid separator is the black turtle's coloration. Black turtles are as dark as their name suggests, having gray, dark gray, or black coloration over their entire body as adults. These turtles are also smaller as adults than are green turtles from other populations, averaging only 155 to 265 lb (70 to 120 kg), and their number of eggs per clutch is also small, averaging about 70. Black turtles have a slightly different shape to their carapace, which is more vaulted and narrower at its rear than in other green turtles, and which has arched indentations over its rear flippers.

Although the physical attributes of black turtles hint that they are distinct from other green turtles, their genes tell us this is not necessarily so. Careful examinations of their genetics reveal that black turtles are no more separated from the global group of green turtle assemblages than are many other populations of green turtles. However, many biologists agree that the black turtle is isolated in its distribution, is significantly different from other populations, and may at least be an incipient species; that is, one that may be in the process of emerging as a unique and reproductively isolated form.

All green turtles have a blunt head and a rounded leading edge to their beak. Their lower jaw sheath is coarsely serrated and has a sharp cusp at its tip. The upper beak has ridges on its inner cutting edge, which with the serrated lower beak make for an efficient set of seagrass clippers. If perturbed, a green turtle may clench its jaws, grinding together the rough edges of its beak to make a creaking sound.

Although a relatively good look at a green turtle is possible in shallow clear waters, a surfacing turtle is likely to offer only a brief glimpse before disappearing beneath a boil. The closest most of us are likely to get to a green turtle is on a nesting beach. On a nesting beach at night, one can identify a green turtle by the silhouette of her domed shell and small head. As adults, green turtles have the smallest head in proportion to their body size of all the sea turtles. But even if one arrives too late to see

The algae growing on a green turtle's shell provide a grazing opportunity for gold-ring surgeonfish living on a Hawaiian reef.

a green turtle attempting to nest, her tracks on the beach are enough to determine that a green turtle has visited. A green turtle's track is a symmetrical series of flipper gouges a little over 3 ft (1 m) in width. Diagonal marks on the track's edge are from the turtle's long front flippers, and parallel marks on either side

Major Nesting Beaches   Large Juveniles & Adults   Oceanic Juveniles

of the midline are from the simultaneous push from the turtle's rear flippers. Along the track center is commonly a pencil-thin tail drag punctuated by points where the turtle rested between each simultaneous heave from her flippers. A green turtle's nest site appears as if it were the result of a subsurface explosion. On soft sand beaches, a nesting green turtle leaves a pit 7 ft (2 m) in diameter and more than 20 in (0.5 m) deep. The pit lies at one end of an oval mound of sand as wide as the pit and up to several feet long.

Distribution and Movements

Green turtles swim in all of the world's warm-water oceans (Atlantic, Indian, and Pacific) and are most common within and just outside of the tropics. Although green turtles are found feeding in shallow waters as far north as Bermuda and as far south as Brisbane, Australia, they are essentially tropical sea turtles. They are known from the waters of roughly 140 countries and have been recorded to nest in 80 of these. Their nesting beaches are also mostly within the tropics, with all of the major nesting beaches lying between latitudes 20° north and south.

Within their global range green turtles make extensive movements but are unlikely to pass between oceans. Green turtles from temperate waters are known to migrate north and south with the seasons, although turtles in more tropical locations may remain within the same waters for years. Females migrating from feeding areas to nesting beaches make the most directed movements. A green turtle migrating to nest may swim dozens of miles a day to reach a familiar 110 yd (100 m) stretch of beach lying 1240 miles (2000 km) or more away from where she feeds.

Life History

Like the other sea turtles, a green turtle begins its life as a hatchling escaping from a sandy nest. After they enter the sea as hatchlings, green turtles are seldom seen until they reappear as dinner-plate sized juveniles swimming in shallow near-shore waters. Their absence during a period of growth out in deep ocean waters has been described as the 'lost year', although biologists now feel that this oceanic stage is probably 2 to 7 years. The size of green turtles when they leave the open ocean is known to be about 8 to 14 in (20 to 35 cm) in shell length, but their rate of growth is unknown, which leaves the precise duration of this oceanic stage a mystery. During the oceanic stage, it is thought that green turtles circle ocean basins riding upon their sluggish swirl of surface currents. It is interesting that Atlantic green turtles exit the open ocean at about 10 in (25 cm) shell length, and Pacific green turtles, which may have circled an ocean twice the size of the Atlantic, do not appear in coastal waters until they are 14 in (35 cm) in shell length.

Green turtles become better known to biologists as they forage on seagrass and algal pastures around islands and within coastal lagoons, bays, and reef tracts. Some juvenile green turtles live in areas where larger green turtles occur, and other green turtles tend to segregate their feeding areas by size. For instance, only juveniles between 8 and 28 in (20 and 70 cm) in shell length are found in shallow Florida coastal waters. Turtles ready to take the next step to maturity apparently leave Florida for the western Caribbean. Green turtles tagged in eastern Florida by Doc Ehrhart and his students at the University of Central Florida have shown up off Nicaragua, where green turtles larger than 28 in (70 cm), including adults, commonly feed on vast seagrass pastures.

A green turtle's growth rate slows greatly as it ages. Its mass increases 100-fold during the turtle's first few years, between hatching and the turtle's return to shallow waters. Over the following two decades or so, a juvenile green turtle's mass will increase about 20-fold. Then, at about half of its adult weight, a green turtle will spend the next two or more decades doubling its mass. At adulthood, growth is almost imperceptible even over periods of many years. Based on rates of growth seen in wild turtles from many locations, green turtles reach mature size in 20 to 50 years – the longest generation time of any of the sea turtles.

Adult females migrate to reproduce about every 2 to 4 years and lay eggs in 1 to 7 nests separated by roughly two-week intervals. Green turtle eggs are white spheres that average

Adult green turtles from the Galapagos are smaller and have darker pigmentation than those from other ocean regions.

about 2 oz (45 g) and produce a hatchling that averages about 1 oz (25 g). The number of eggs in a green turtle's clutch varies between populations, mostly according to the sizes of nesting females. A population with females maturing at a small size (for example, 30 in /80 cm in shell length) may average only 80 eggs per clutch, whereas a population with larger females (45 in / 115 cm shell length) may average 145 eggs per clutch. Males generally intercept females to mate along migration pathways or just off the nesting beach.

Green turtles are the lawn mowers of the sea.
They maintain close-cropped plots of seagrass that are more productive
and more nutritious than that of ungrazed areas.

Diet

Green turtles begin their lives as omnivores feeding opportunistically in the open ocean. There are few observations indicating what the smallest green turtles feed on. In young-of-the-year turtles that had been swept by tropical storms onto Florida's Atlantic coast, little green turtles were found to have eaten plants and animals, including tiny hydroids, crustaceans, bryozoans, and algae that are common from the floating patches of golden sargasso weed adrift in the Atlantic's currents. Slightly larger green turtles, those that have grown to nearly 8 in (20 cm) in carapace length but still bear the brilliant white plastron of an oceanic turtle, are occasionally found with open-ocean animals such as by-the-wind sailors (*Velella*, a colonial hydroid) and purple sea snails (*Janthina*) in their stomachs.

When they settle into shallow coastal waters, green turtles take up a vegetarian diet. As herbivores, green turtles feed on a wide variety of algal and seagrass species. A rich community of microbes that they maintain in their gut aids their digestion of this plant material. Like animals that graze on land, green turtles are not able to break down the polymer chains of plant cellulose, and without the tiny symbiotic organisms living within them, they would starve. The bacterial and protozoan gut flora of green turtles is thought to be specific to the cellulose of particular plant groups. Thus, individual green turtles are often found to specialize on only algae or on only seagrasses.

Green turtles in the wild eat little animal material, but occasionally take in sponges and small invertebrates that might be consumed incidentally. However, when given the opportunity to eat animals in captivity, green turtles can survive for years on nothing else. Growth rates for green turtles fed fish and squid in captivity are apparently higher than in the wild, but such a high-protein diet has been seen to bring about pathological conditions and occasional death.

Unique Traits

Green turtles are fast, agile swimmers and may be the swiftest of all the sea turtles. Their speed is such that a powerboat might have difficulty keeping up with a small green turtle even in clear shallow water. They startle easily, and when chased, a green turtle the size of a large Frisbee can surpass 12 miles (20 km) per hour, porpoise from the water during breaths, and dart at sharp angles to instantaneously change its direction. Especially in young green turtles, their seabottom-colored camouflage, vigorous swimming, and propensity to startle, reflect an animal that is probably exposed to occasional risks from large predators.

The excitability of a juvenile green turtle in the water belies its behavior when brought aboard a boat. Taken from their element, other sea turtles can be expected to crawl about, flap, and make attempts to bite their captors. But a captured green turtle quickly becomes calm and submissive, resting upon the deck with a bowed head while biologists make their measurements. Green turtles almost never attempt to bite the hand that studies them. But their serenity ends when they are brought near the water for their release. The sendoff typically results in an explosion of flapping and spray as the turtle enters the water.

Individuals in some green turtle populations show a behavioral trait that is unique among the sea turtles; they crawl upon land in daylight to bask. It is a trait seen only in turtles living around remote islands such as the Galapagos, Australia's Bountiful Island in the Gulf of Carpentaria, and the westernmost islands of the Hawaiian archipelago. Although it is not known exactly why green turtles bask, or why individuals from most populations do not, it is easy to see how the trait would be relegated to places that were only rarely visited by humans. Serenely soaking up sunshine on a beach is a behavior that would have been rapidly extinguished as the local native people partook of the easy harvest.

Conservation Status

We have only guesses about the historical abundance of green turtles, but they are believed to have been one of the most common large animals on the planet. Today, they are much more rare following profoundly rapid declines. Green turtles have been eaten by people for thousands of years, but we can be relatively

This tiny hatchling green turtle will not reach adulthood for about 30 years.

sure that the last few hundred years have taken the greatest toll on green turtles. Over this period, human population growth, technological advancement, and a specific taste for green turtles have led to a high risk of green turtles becoming extinct.

The carrying capacity of the Caribbean's seagrass pastures suggests that 30 to 40 million adult green turtles once filled this sea. But even if this estimate is high, harvest records of green turtles kept by Europeans reveal that they drew from a Caribbean population of at least a few million individuals. Today, only a thin fraction of this abundance remains.

Green turtles worldwide are depleted and most populations are continuing to decline. A recent global assessment of the green turtle by Jeff Seminoff describes how the world's green turtle population has declined by about half over the last three generations (about 140 years). Some populations have declined over 90 per cent during this period and several green turtle rookeries have been extirpated.

Some green turtle populations measured at their nesting beaches have been protected from harvest and are now beginning to show signs of recovery. But superimposed on our attempts to protect green turtles are numerous threats that have only been recognized recently. One of these new threats is a mysterious skin-tumor disease called fibropapillomatosis. In specific locations that are now spread throughout the turtle's range, green turtles have been appearing with warty growths as large as grapefruit on their skin and eyes. Such individuals frequently become entangled in debris, starve to death, or succumb to associated internal tumors that crowd major organs and blood vessels. A herpes-like virus is thought to cause the tumors, but the role of the turtle's environment in making them susceptible to the virus remains unclear.

The green turtle is considered by the IUCN, The World Conservation Union, to be Endangered. This status means that they face a very high risk of extinction in the wild in the near future, with 'very high risk' and 'near future' defined in terms of percent population decline over time measured in green turtle generations.

Green turtles were formerly one of the most common large animals on Earth.

Loggerhead Sea Turtle

Scientific Name

Caretta caretta.
New Latin modification of the French word *caret* for turtle.

Other common names

Other English names include loggerhead, loggerhead seaturtle, and logrit (Caribbean). In Latin America, common names include caguama and cabezona (Spanish). Many other common names vary among cultures.

Size and weight

Adult female loggerheads weigh between 155 and 375 lb (70 and 170 kg), with a shell straight-length of 30 to 43 in (80 to 110 cm). Adult males are slightly larger than females.

Distribution

Warm temperate marine waters and into the tropics, but only occasionally found within 8 degrees of the equator. Most nesting occurs on warm temperate beaches or just inside the tropics.

General Appearance

Much of a loggerhead's appearance gives the impression of a tough, worn, weathered brute of a turtle. If the smooth, rounded, unfettered form of a green turtle can be said to be feminine, then a typical loggerhead, scarred, notched, and bedecked with barnacles, might be described as having a decidedly masculine roughness around the edges. Yet, many would argue that loggerheads have a noble beauty all their own.

The coloration of an adult loggerhead's shell is often partially obscured by a carpet of macroalgae, large barnacles, and a varied host of clinging tagalongs. Where the shell is visible, it is dark reddish brown. On close examination, the brown color can be seen to come from a radiating pattern of orange, red, brown, and black smears within each shell scute. The shell scutes are frequently fragmented and peeling where many old thin layers of keratin flake away as new scutes grow from underneath. At whatever rate a loggerhead is able to shed its acquired load of commensal organisms by losing its shell scutes, it is not frequent enough to keep many loggerheads from looking much like the seabottom they rest on.

The scales atop the head of a loggerhead typically take the reddish-brown coloration of the turtle's shell, although the sides of the head and neck are nearly always a bright golden yellow. This same yellow coloration covers the shoulders and the entire underside of the turtle. The upper surfaces of the flippers have coin-sized scales that are most frequently orange-brown and outlined in yellow.

The loggerhead's shell is a stout wedge shape with a width about three-quarters its length. Loggerheads have five lateral scutes on either side of their carapace midline. On the head, loggerheads are distinguished from other sea turtles in having two pairs of prefrontal scales between the eyes, which often have one or two intervening scales.

The loggerhead's massive head is its namesake. The width of the average head is often substantially larger than our own. A loggerhead's upper jaw sheath is highly thickened, with a curved leading edge and a blunt cusp. The lower jaw is sheathed in equally thick keratin and has a broad crushing surface at its cusped end. Bulging jowls betray a robust machinery of bony framework and muscle for pulverizing the hardest of mollusk

Adult loggerhead sea turtles feed on slow-moving, hard-shelled animals and reach an average weight of about 240 lb (110 kg).

shells. A perturbed loggerhead will occasionally grind its jaws and produce a sound like the creaking of a strained timber.

Hatchlings are about 2 in (4.5 cm) in shell length. Their coloration varies greatly from light (tan or pale gray) to dark (brown, charcoal, or black). Most hatchlings are countershaded light below and dark above, but others may be uniformly pigmented. The trailing margins of the shell and flippers are often lighter than

Loggerhead hatchlings vary in coloration from blonde to black.

the hatchlings' background color. The lightest hatchlings often have darker centers to their cheek scutes, giving them a freckled look. The carapace is lumpy with the raised scutes that will later become thickened keels as hatchlings grow into juveniles.

As a young loggerhead grows to be larger than a handful, its carapace and other dorsal scutes take on an orange-brown color with faint patterns of radiating streaks within each scute. Their lower surfaces become amber yellow, the hue of vibrant *Sargassum* weed. During the first half of their development, a period that corresponds with life in the open ocean, juvenile loggerheads bear thick, rear-pointing spiny keels on their shell. Three keels above and

two below, in addition to serrations at the rear margins of the shell, must make a young loggerhead a tough target for oceanic sharks.

Larger juveniles, those greater than 18 in (45 cm) shell length, have begun to grow out of their thickened shell scutes. Toward adulthood, their shells elongate, scutes become thinner and flaky, marginal serrations disappear, and the only remaining topography to the shell is a pronounced hump toward the rear over the turtle's sequestered hips. Larger immatures and adults also differ from small juveniles in having three thickened traction scales on the underside of each rear flipper and two to three similarly callused scales under the wrists of their fore-flippers. These scales are testimony to the propensity of larger loggerheads to occupy shallow waters where they crawl along the seabottom.

A casual observer seeing a loggerhead breathe at the surface will recognize the turtle by its large golden and orange-brown head. On occasion, mariners may have the opportunity to pass closely by a loggerhead seemingly sleeping at the surface. There, an observer can be relatively certain that a large-headed orange and brown turtle with scattered barnacles is a loggerhead. On a nesting beach at night, a female loggerhead can be identified by the silhouette of her somewhat straight-backed shell and large head. The track left by a nesting loggerhead is an asymmetrical series of paisley swirls from the rear flippers on either side of a flat, smooth, wavy center mark. A typical track is a little less than 3 ft (1 m) in width and is usually without a tail drag down the center. A loggerhead's nest is generally a 7 ft (2 m) wide circular mound of sand next to a slightly smaller hemispherical pit. Loggerhead nest pits and mounds are much less extensive than those at green turtle nest sites.

Distribution and Movements

Loggerhead sea turtles inhabit the temperate and tropical waters of the Atlantic, Indian, and Pacific oceans. Their foraging range during the summer months extends well into New England in

North America, although the species is most common between latitudes 40 degrees north and south. Loggerheads are rare in the central tropics. Nesting beaches are distributed throughout roughly 50 countries but about 80–90 percent of nesting occurs in only two, the United States (southeast only) and Oman (mostly the island of Masirah).

The greatest voyages made by loggerheads are when they are small. Because these turtles spend such a long time as juveniles out in the open ocean (about a decade), they have ample opportunities for travel. Researchers believe that little loggerheads may travel tens of thousands of kilometers around their ocean's basin before they settle into a life closer to shore. Like other sea turtles from temperate waters, loggerheads tend to migrate north and south with the seasons, but turtles in warmer waters may stay put throughout the year. Females migrate from their feeding areas, which are typically located in subtropical waters, to nesting beaches lining more temperate regions.

Life History

Loggerhead hatchlings dispersing from their natal beaches begin an open-ocean life stage that lasts from 7 to 12 years. During this time young loggerheads feed near the surface and do a great deal of floating while ocean currents disperse them. But in-between bouts of laziness, young loggerheads can be surprisingly active.

Oceanic juvenile loggerheads large enough to require two hands to lift have been tracked using satellite transmitters attached by researchers working in the central Pacific and in the eastern Atlantic near the Azores and Madeira. In the persistent eddies that occur near the Azores, loggerheads were found

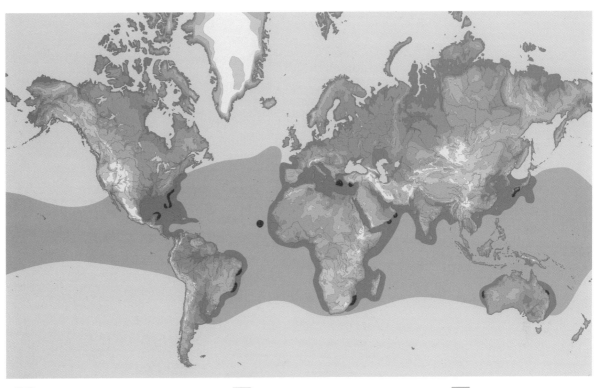

■ *Major Nesting Beaches*   ■ *Large Juveniles & Adults*   ■ *Oceanic Juveniles*

to linger for months within the swirling waters above regional sea mounts waiting to become islands. Although the Azorean loggerheads spent 80 per cent of their time within 16 ft (5 m) of the surface and seldom averaged greater swimming than 800 yd (750 m) per hour, turtles would occasionally dive to 330 ft (100 m) or more. At Madeira, loggerheads were found to be more directed in their swimming and to eventually move far westward from where they were first satellite tagged. In the central Pacific, loggerheads were tracked as they moved along

A loggerhead sea turtle in shallow Bahamian waters crushes a
tulip shell formerly protecting a hermit crab. These turtles are able to feed on
a variety of hard-shelled animals that are armored against most predators.

oceanic fronts lying between water masses of high and low concentrations of plankton. In all cases, it seems that little loggerheads in the open ocean position themselves or are carried by currents into concentrations of floating and subsurface food in the open ocean.

From growth studies done by Karen Bjorndal and Alan Bolten of loggerheads at sea, it is apparent that they outgrow their ability to forage efficiently in the open ocean. The largest oceanic loggerheads have lower growth rates than do similar-sized loggerheads that have shifted to coastal foraging. So it seems that a loggerhead's dramatic change in habitat is driven by food opportunities. Although the wide ocean's surface may suit little loggerheads that can survive off the small drifting creatures swept into oceanic fronts, larger loggerheads require more substantial meals that can only be easily found only in shallower coastal waters.

Loggerheads settling into shallow waters near coastlines inhabit lagoons, bays, channels, and reefs ranging in depth from 330 ft (100 m) deep to less than 3 ft (1 m). As in green turtles, these larger juveniles may live for many years in habitats and regions where no adolescent or adult turtles are found. Nearing maturity, many loggerheads migrate closer to the tropics and reach pubescence and adulthood far from where they first encountered shallow water as juveniles.

Estimating from the rate at which loggerheads grow, adult size is reached in roughly 20 to 40 years. As in most other sea turtles, adult loggerheads nearly stop growing such that adult turtles observed over 20 years scarcely change in size beyond the error range in their shell measurement. From hatchling to adult, a loggerhead multiplies its mass by a little over 6000 times.

Female loggerheads migrate to breed at their nesting beaches about every two to four years and lay eggs in one to seven nests separated by roughly two-week intervals. Their eggs average about 1 oz (33 g) and a hatchling fresh from the nest is about 1/2 oz (20 g). The number of eggs in a loggerhead's clutch is fairly constant between populations, averaging about 115. Males generally intercept females to mate along migration pathways and are seldom seen near the nesting beach.

Diet

Loggerheads take their first bite of food out in the open ocean and their early tastes are not discriminating. A little loggerhead's meals are likely to include hundreds of items found amongst the patches of algae and flotsam they live by, including plants, invertebrate animals, dead insects, and many other slow-moving and inanimate things. As oceanic loggerheads grow, they become able to catch larger prey, but they remain dependant upon sluggish sea creatures such as jellyfish, salps (translucent, free-swimming sea squirts), floating sea snails, and goose-neck barnacles.

Juvenile and adult loggerheads that have begun feeding in shallow coastal waters eat a wide variety of local seafood. Although preferred species vary by region, typical loggerhead food consists of large, bottom-crawling or attached, hard-shelled invertebrates like marine snails, clams, non-swimming crabs, and sea pens (pen-like colonies of coral-related animals). Occasionally, loggerheads eat softer foods such as jellyfish, sea squirts, and anemones.

Unique Traits

To catch their food, loggerheads are known to muscle through whatever obstacle keeps them from their prey. This means mashing a wooden-slatted trap to bits in pursuit of a captive spiny lobster, consuming the sponge and coral concealing a cowering crab, and flipper-plowing through bottom sediment to get at burrowing bivalve mollusks.

Loggerheads do not swim as swiftly as the other sea turtle species. They are mild-mannered creatures, but if directly confronted with a threat, they are not shy about using the crushing power of their enormous jaws. In responses to the unwelcome attention from a potential predator or to the competing affections offered by a rival male, a loggerhead's tendency is to bite decisively and let go eventually.

Conservation Status

This captive loggerhead participated in tests of turtle excluder devices (TEDs).

There are only two places in the world where loggerheads breed in abundance. One area is along the southern Florida Peninsula, USA, and the other is on Masirah Island, Oman. Elsewhere, loggerhead nesting is much less common, even rare, and many of these smaller populations are in perilous decline.

Loggerheads in the Pacific are in particular trouble. In about a generation, nesting loggerheads in Japan are down to about 10 per cent of their numbers when counts first began. And in Queensland, Australia, nesting loggerheads have declined to about 14 per cent of their abundance only half a generation ago. In Florida, the loggerhead population once thought of as stable has begun to decline. In Oman, uncertainties over trends in nesting numbers leave it unclear how loggerheads there are doing.

In general, loggerheads have not suffered from the intense commercial harvests that some other sea turtle species have experienced. But this does not mean that loggerheads have avoided human threats. This species has had the misfortune of positioning itself between us and the seafood we wish to harvest. Juvenile loggerheads forage and float precisely where long-lines (series of baited hooks) are set to catch oceanic fishes, and larger loggerheads feed within areas of fertile seabottom trawled for shrimps (prawns). At these intersections, loggerheads perish by the tens of thousands each year after being hooked, tangled, and drowned. Good news for loggerheads and other sea turtles is that progress is being made to reduce this mortality by modifying the gear that fishermen use. Unfortunately, open ocean fisheries lag far behind in this effort compared to coastal fisheries. Although the threats per hook and per trawl have great potential to be reduced, the overall number of hooks and trawls is increasing. This leaves the fate of the world's loggerheads in question.

The loggerhead sea turtle is considered by the IUCN to be Endangered. This status means that loggerheads face a very high risk of extinction in the wild in the near future.

The distributions of loggerheads and humans commonly intersect. Loggerheads are frequently tangled, hooked, and drowned by commercial fishing operations, and are struck and crushed by vessels and dredges.

Hawksbill Turtle

Scientific Name

Eretmochelys imbricata.
Named for the Greek roots for 'rowing turtle' (turtle with oars) and the Latin root for 'covered with overlapping scales' (likely pertaining to the hawksbill's overlapping shell scutes).

Other common names

Other English names given the hawksbill turtle include hawksbill sea turtle, hawksbill, and hawksbill seaturtle. In Latin America, the turtle is known most often as carey (kä-râ'). Many other common names vary among cultures.

Size and weight

Adult female hawksbills weigh between 88 and 176 lb (40 and 80 kg), with a shell straight-length of 30 to 35 in (75 to 90 cm).

Distribution

Tropical marine waters of the Atlantic, Pacific and Indian oceans. Nesting occurs almost exclusively on tropical beaches. Mexico, the Seychelles, Indonesia and Australia have the most significant nesting beaches, although they breed on beaches of about 60 countries.

General Appearance

Hawksbills are strikingly beautiful turtles. Although much of their beauty lies in their intricately patterned shell, a hawksbill's flippers and head also reflect the theme of colors that the turtles carry on their backs. A hawksbill's shell colors seem magnified, perhaps by the thickness of the translucent scutes covering their carapace. The tough, plastic-like scute plates are as thick as about 20 of these book pages and are imbedded with a myriad of colors. From a distance, hawksbill shells range in appearance from blonde with chocolate drippings to black with golden sunbursts. Up close in daylight, a hawksbill shell can be seen to have colors such as cream, amber, rusty reds, browns, and black, occasionally all together, in rich patterns ranging from overlapping bursts and radiating zigzags, to irregular superimposed splotches. Given this variation, no two hawksbills are quite the same.

Typically, a hawksbills underside is much paler than its topside. In many young hawksbills, the scutes covering the plastron are a patternless, thick cream color, although these belly scutes may have dark corners in some turtles. In adults, the plastron becomes a deep amber. Depending on the life experiences of an individual turtle, some of the beauty of a hawksbill's shell may be hidden by coarse sandpaper-like scratches from rocks and coral.

Hawksbill shell scutes are imbricate, meaning that each slightly overlaps the scute behind it. The center-line vertebral scutes overlap the most, such that they taper rearward into sharp Vs or Ws. Faster-growing young hawksbills have the sharpest rear margins to each of their imbricate scutes.

Young hawksbills have a heart-shaped shell with sharply serrate rear margins. In oceanic-stage turtles, the shell appears lumpy from the thickened scutes that form three longitudinal ridges on the carapace and two on the plastron. Hawksbills larger than a shovelhead have only a hint of these ridges. As hawksbills age into maturity, their shell elongates, and in the oldest individuals, the shell is smooth and the serrate rear margins have largely worn away.

The head and flipper scales of a hawksbill keep with the general color theme of the carapace but are likely to show greater

Adult hawksbills feed mostly on sponges and reach an average weight of about 150 lb (70 kg).

contrast. Frequently, an amber background separates dark-brown scale centers. Darker colors are much more dominant in the upper surfaces than they are beneath.

Hawksbill turtles have four lateral scutes on either side of their carapace midline. On the head, hawksbills are similar to loggerheads in having two pairs of prefrontal scales between the eyes, often with an intervening scale or two.

*A hawksbill's narrow beak and long neck allow
it to probe reef crevasses for food.*

A narrow raptor-like beak is the hawksbill's namesake. With the slightly cusped bill arching into an overbite and extending about half the length of the head, the turtle's profile is decidedly bird-like. The beak is strong, sharp, slender, and in a form designed for probing and extraction from the stony crevices of coral reefs. Hawksbills also have a longer neck than the other sea turtles, which may allow an extended reach into a reef's more secluded spots.

Hatchlings are about 2 in (4 cm) in shell length. Their coloration varies between light and dark, and browns and grays. Most hatchlings are slightly lighter below. Their carapace has the three thin longitudinal ridges that will thicken as they grow at sea.

In a cursory glimpse of a hawksbill from the water's surface, one could easily make identification from the head profile and shell colors. In the water, the same characters give the turtle away, but noting the presence of the turtle's sharply overlapping shell scutes can make a confirmation. Older hawksbills have often collected a scattering of large *Chelonibia* barnacles but are not often as fouled as a typical loggerhead.

Hawksbills nesting on beaches are not readily observed and commonly leave only obscure traces. Often, the only evidence from a nesting is a short track disappearing into thick beach vegetation. Hawksbills leave an asymmetrical series of flipper prints in the sand spanning about 2 ft (0.75 m), typically with a zigzagging tail-drag mark down the center of the track. Their nests are a pit with an adjacent mound 5 ft (1.5 m) or so in width, but this evidence is frequently obscured by dune undergrowth and beach wrack.

Distribution and Movements

Hawksbills are largely restricted to the tropics and are known from the Atlantic, Indian, and Pacific oceans. Their distribution in the water mirrors the distribution of the planet's great coral reefs. Although immature hawksbills do wander between reef sites, it is unlikely that these movements are seasonal. Although it was once thought that hawksbills migrated little after settling into coastal waters, we now know that they make punctuated shifts between habitats similar to other species of sea turtles. Hawksbills are observed again and again over many years resting under the same coral ledge but are also known to travel hundreds of miles between reef habitats. Adult hawksbills may forage within 60 miles (100 km) of the beaches where they nest, or they may travel as far as 1240 miles (2000 km) between their foraging and breeding sites.

Nesting occurs principally on island beaches and is far more scattered than in the other sea turtle species. Although hawksbills breed on the beaches of about 60 countries, none has any great concentration of this activity. Mexico, Seychelles, Indonesia, and Australia have the most significant nesting of hawksbill turtles. The largest population of nesting hawksbills may be at Milman Island, within Australia's northern Great Barrier Reef.

Small oceanic hawksbills drift in ocean currents but are seldom known to cross entire oceans. Larger juveniles and adults spend most of their lives in waters less than 100 ft (30 m) deep and may frequent habitat that is barely wet at low tide.

Life History

Hawksbills leave their natal beaches as hatchlings and disperse into oceanic waters where they are believed to forage within surface weedlines. Because hawksbills appear in shallow coastal waters when their shells are only 8 to 12 in (20 to 30 cm) in length, they are thought to spend only a few years out in the open ocean.

Young hawksbills just entering coastal waters have a limited band of suitable reef habitats dotting the tropics and near-tropics. Thus, it would seem to behoove a little hawksbill not to stray too far into temperate waters as they are carried within ocean currents. Although it is uncertain how long little hawksbills spend in the open ocean, the small size at which they leave this habitat suggests that

their oceanic stage is vastly reduced in comparison to loggerheads, as is the risk of being carried too far from tropical waters.

Juvenile hawksbills settling into coastal waters occupy reefs of all kinds. Although living corals are not a requirement for hawksbill habitat, they do characterize the reefs where hawksbills are most

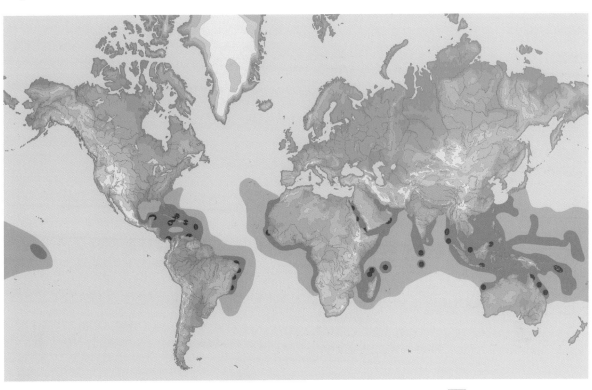

■ *Major Nesting Beaches*   ■ *Large Juveniles & Adults*   ■ *Oceanic Juveniles*

commonly found. In addition to favoring the organisms on which hawksbills feed, the hard and irregular features of reefs also provide ledges and caves within which hawksbills rest and avoid predators.

Just outside the tropics, there are areas of hardbottom and coral reef where mostly juvenile hawksbills are found. But within the tropics, deep hawksbill habitat often has a complete array of hawksbill sizes from plate-sized juveniles to full-sized adults. Growth of hawksbills from hatchling to adult is thought to take 20 to 40 years. Female hawksbills migrate to breed at their nesting

beaches about every two to four years. Hawksbill nesting often has a peak during the rainy season but could occur throughout the year. During a nesting season, most hawksbills will put an average of 130, 1-oz (27-g) eggs into each of two to four nests. Successive nestings are separated by intervals of about two weeks. Eggs incubate roughly 60 days before hatchlings emerge from the nest. Hatchlings average about 1/2 oz (15 g).

Diet

Although the diet of little hawksbills living in the open ocean is uncertain, these smallest hawksbills are thought to feed on surface-drifting organisms just as the youngest loggerheads do. Soon after settling onto shallow reefs, juvenile hawksbills are thought to undergo a profound transition in diet. Although some of the smallest coastal hawksbills are found to eat a wide variety of invertebrate animals and algae, most juveniles and adults assume a more parochial diet. For most of their lives, hawksbills are spongivores – specialists on eating sponges.

Sponges are an unusual food choice in that they possess substantial defenses against would-be predators. By lacing themselves with toxic chemicals and dangerously indigestible silica spicules, many sponges are not the favored item on most animal menus. Yet, hawksbills quickly acquire a taste and tolerance for sponge, and after a short initiation period, sponges are likely to make up 95 per cent of their diet. A limited number of species belonging to the order of demosponges are the hawksbill's favorites. Although this is the order that gives us the familiar bath sponge, these friendly and caressing sponges made of flexible spongin are generally shunned by hawksbills. Many of the sponges eaten by hawksbills are held together by lacy, glass-like silica that you would no more want near your bare skin than shredded glass.

A hawksbill's tolerance for a diet of glass is largely a mystery. Occasionally, hawksbills do eat less toxic fare such as sea cucumbers, mollusks, anemones, sea urchins, crabs, and algae, but

Hawksbills have an amazing ability to eat and digest toxic sponges.

the rarity of these substitutes points to a clear preference for sponges. It is a wonder what benefit from eating sponge could possibly outweigh the difficulties of such a diet.

Unique Traits

Hawksbills are nimble turtles that seem unafraid of obstacles. At home on the reef, they are commonly found wedged into

As protection against the many rough, pointed, and stinging features of a coral reef, hawksbills have thick shell coverings and tough skin.

crevasses and beneath ledges from which they seem barely able to extricate themselves. Perhaps more than the other sea turtles, hawksbills make a practice of jamming themselves into tight spots and knocking about on rough, wave-swept reefs. One function of a hawksbill's thick shell scutes may be to protect them from the jabs they are likely to get as they poke about the sharp corals and rocky projections looking for the next meal of

Hawksbill hatchlings on a Mona Island beach in the Caribbean.

sponge. It is a protection needed especially by nesting female hawksbills, which occasionally crawl over the gothic projections of fringing reef to access a sandy beach. Once on a beach, hawksbills are even less intimidated by the tangle of branches and vines on the upper beach where eggs can incubate away from the tide. Hawksbills probably surpass the other sea turtles in their maneuverability on land, and are able to employ a tactic largely unheard of for a sea turtle out of its element – hawksbills can back up.

Conservation Status

The best guesses of biologists are that the world's hawksbills have declined by 80 per cent or more during the past century. Given the direction of current population trends and the continuation of threats faced by hawksbills, most believe that this slide toward extinction will be difficult to reverse. Because hawksbills are widespread in the tropics there is an illusion that the species is holding its own. But most of these populations are either declining or are mere shadows of their former abundance. Fewer than 15,000 females nest on beaches worldwide each year, and this nesting is stretched between hundreds of small and vulnerable nesting populations. The Caribbean now has about a third of the world's hawksbill nesting. In this region, one possible bright spot is the Yucatan Peninsula of Mexico where about a thousand hawksbills nest each year and where the nesting trend seems to be increasing.

Like the green turtle, the hawksbill has suffered the fate of a commercially harvested species. For many decades, hawksbills have been harvested for their shell scutes. These scutes as a trade commodity are known as tortoiseshell, bekko, or carey. The malleable, plastic-like plates are fashioned into jewelry, hair combs, eyeglass frames, and varied ornaments. Shell scutes from 30,000 or more hawksbills per year were imported into Japan alone during the period of 1970 to 1992. Currently, trade in tortoiseshell has diminished following adherence to an international convention (CITES) to protect endangered species, but substantial illegal harvest and trade still occurs. Domestic harvest of hawksbills remains common in Fiji, the Solomon Islands, Cambodia, Indonesia, the Dominican Republic, Cuba and throughout Central America.

The hawksbill is considered by IUCN to be Critically Endangered. This status means that hawksbills face an extremely high risk of extinction in the wild in the immediate future.

Unfortunately for hawksbills, their beautiful shell scutes, known as tortoiseshell, are used to make commercial products and ornaments.

Olive Ridley

Scientific Name

Lepidochelys olivacea.

Named for the Greek roots for 'scaly turtle' (perhaps from the turtle's extra carapace scutes) and the Latin root for 'olive-like' (likely pertaining to the turtle's coloration).

Other common names

Other English names given the olive ridley include olive ridley sea turtle, olive ridley seaturtle, Pacific ridley, and olive loggerhead. In Latin America, the turtle is known most often as tortuga golfina. Many other common names vary among cultures.

Size and weight

Adult female olive ridleys weigh between 77 and 100 lb (35 and 45 kg), with a shell straight-length of 25 to 30 in (60 to 75 cm).

Distribution

Tropical marine waters of the Atlantic, Pacific and Indian oceans. Nesting occurs on beaches mostly in the tropics. In the eastern Pacific they nest on several beaches in Mexico and Central America, but are almost completely absent from islands in the central Pacific. In the Indian ocean they nest in large numbers only in eastern India and Sri Lanka. Occasional nesting in the Atlantic occurs in Brazil and Western Africa.

General Appearance

The ridleys are the smallest sea turtles. Each of the two species has a relatively large head with a cusped upper beak and each has a heart-shaped, almost circular shell. In a head-on view of an olive ridley, one can see the vaulting of that circular shell, topped by a flat peak and looking overall a bit like a 1950s representation of a flying saucer.

The topsides of olive ridleys tend to be the drab color that their name suggests, but they can also show an overall gray, brown, or black coloration. The underside of an adult is generally yellow. Smaller juveniles are pure white beneath and hatchlings are most commonly gray to black overall.

One unusual character shown by olive ridleys is a tendency toward having extra shell scutes. The number of plates on an olive ridley's back is greater and more variable than the number covering either Kemp's ridley or the other sea turtles. Most olive ridleys have six to nine pairs of lateral scutes on either side of their carapace midline (Kemp's ridleys typically have five pairs), and some turtles may have one or more lateral scutes on one side than on the other. Most olive ridleys also have six to nine vertebral scutes along the midline length of their shell (Kemp's ridleys generally have five vertebral scutes). In additional comparisons to Kemp's ridley, olive ridleys have a slightly more triangular head, subtly larger eyes, and a shell that has both less breadth and more height.

Another character of both ridley species is the presence of four conspicuous pore openings on each side of their lower shell. The pores are openings for the mysterious Rathke's glands (also present but inconspicuous in hawksbills and green turtles), which may secrete pheromones or anti-fouling substances, or perform some other function that has thus far escaped the imaginations of biologists.

Because ridleys are small, they leave fainter tracks on nesting beaches than the other sea turtles. Having emerged onto a beach, ridleys leave an asymmetrical series of swirls from the rear

Adult olive ridleys feed on a variety of hard- and soft-bodied invertebrates and reach an average weight of about 90 lb (40 kg).

flippers on either side of a flat, smooth, wavy center mark. A typical track is a little less than 2 ft (0.66 m) in width and has no tail drag mark down the center.

Distribution and Movements

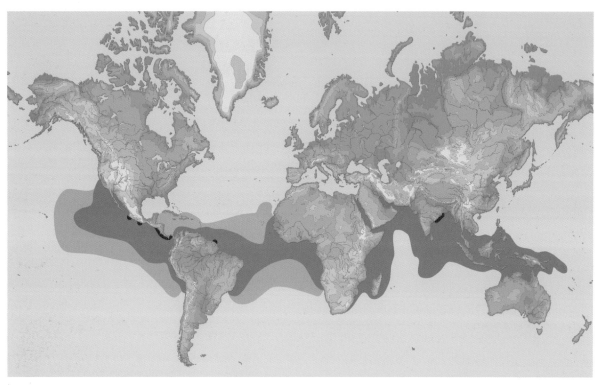

■ *Major Nesting Beaches* ■ *Large Juveniles & Adults* ■ *Oceanic Juveniles*

Olive ridleys are almost exclusively tropical sea turtles. They occur in Pacific, Indian, and Atlantic oceans, but their distribution is patchy. In the eastern Pacific, olive ridleys nest in impressive numbers on several Mexican and Central American beaches. Elsewhere in the Pacific they nest in low numbers, and they are almost completely absent from the islands of the central Pacific. In the Indian Ocean, olive ridleys nest in abundance only in eastern India and Sri Lanka. In the Atlantic, olive ridleys are uncommon, although they were formerly abundant nesters on the

Guianas Coast (Guyana, Surinam, and French Guiana). Occasional nesting in the Atlantic occurs in Brazil and western Africa.

Hatchling olive ridleys enter the sea and are presumed to disperse with oceanic currents. Only rarely are small juvenile olive ridleys observed at sea. But there are occasional sightings of juveniles at the surface of the open ocean having shell-lengths between 8 and 24 in (20 and 60 cm), which suggest that olive ridleys have a multi-year early oceanic stage similar to loggerheads.

Most of what is known about movements of olive ridleys comes from studies of adult female turtles approached by researchers on nesting beaches. At the well-studied beaches of Pacific Costa Rica, tens of thousands of adult female olive ridleys have been tagged with flipper tags so that their identities would be known if the turtles were seen again far from their nesting beach. The locations where these tagged turtles have been recovered are a function of both where the turtles go and where they are likely to be recognized by someone. As it turns out, the vast majority of tag recoveries of these Costa Rican nesters were made as the turtles traveled south, to the waters of coastal Ecuador, where hundreds of thousands of adult olive ridleys were harvested in the 1970s to be turned into leather boots and handbags.

Better detail on movements has come from turtles equipped with radio transmitters capable of delivering location data to orbiting satellites. Tracks of these turtles show them leaving the

Olive ridleys commonly forage near the surface
in deep oceanic waters where they are attracted to floating debris.
They seldom stray outside the tropics.

This female laying her eggs at sunset on a beach
in Surinam is one of few olive ridleys remaining in a western Atlantic
population that is close to regional extirpation.

Pacific waters near their Costa Rica nesting beaches and traveling north to Mexico, south to Peru, and west into the Pacific as far as 1800 miles (3000 km) from land. Most of these adult olive ridleys appeared to be nomadic and did not remain within a single foraging area.

Sometimes, olive ridleys travel within large flotillas. Such aggregations suggest social relations that are unusual for turtles, but they reveal a tendency to group that might be expected from a turtle that assembles in mass *arribadas* during nesting.

Life History

Olive ridleys may spend nearly all of their youth, perhaps a decade or more, out in the open ocean. This remoteness in their lives adds mystery to how they go about living them. We do not know how quickly olive ridleys grow, and we do not know exactly how long they take to reach maturity.

Adulthood is reached at about 24 to 28 in (60 to 70 cm) in shell length. As adults, olive ridleys spend at least some time in coastal waters where they feed on bottom-dwelling creatures. Even in shallow waters near land, olive ridleys seem to show no allegiance to specific home foraging grounds. Often, olive ridleys are observed to be associated with transitory upwelling events that provide pulses of nutrients and explosions of life. They also are found foraging among rafts of floating debris drifting in ocean currents. Because these ridley 'smorgasbords' either grow or assemble, fade or disperse, and then appear again elsewhere, reliance on these events would seem to require a life spent wandering.

Reproduction occurs either within mass *arribadas* or as solitary nestings. Within populations of sufficient size, perhaps hundreds, most female ridleys choose to nest in the company of others.

An individual olive ridley is likely to nest one to three times in a season, with each nest containing approximately 100 to 115 eggs that each weighs about 1 1/4 oz (35 g). The period between successive nests is about 14 days when a turtle nests by herself but can be as long as 48 days for females holding their clutches of eggs for *arribada* events. It is likely that olive ridleys nest almost every year. Hatchlings emerge from nests in 50 to 70 days and weigh approximately 1/2 oz (17 g).

Diet

Olive ridleys eat a wide variety of invertebrate animals from a range of ocean habitats. This diet includes oceanic animals such as pelagic red crabs, jellyfish, salps, and flotsam-attached barnacles, and it includes bottom-dwelling animals like crabs, mollusks, sea urchins, sea squirts, and shrimps. Various algae are eaten, either incidentally or deliberately, and on occasion, benthic fishes are found in the stomachs of olive ridleys stranded dead. Some of these fishes may be eaten as carrion, perhaps being discards from near-shore shrimp trawling. Frequently, olive ridleys become hooked on pelagic long-line fishing gear that has been baited with fish or squid.

Unique Traits

Ridleys may be the most social sea turtles. The behavior that best shows their gregarious nature is the *arribada*. For olive ridleys, these mass nesting events occur at night, which contrasts with the daytime *arribadas* of Kemp's ridley. Olive ridley *arribadas* may involve just a few hundred females nesting on one or two consecutive nights, or they may involve hundreds of thousands of females nesting over several nights. At Orissa, on India's northeast coast, approximately 600,000 turtles once nested in a single week-long *arribada*. Despite the size of the mass-nesting events at Orissa, the normally annual phenomenon was conspicuously absent for two recent years following severe erosion of the nesting beaches. As beaches re-formed, mass nesting returned. Such intensive synchronous nesting, unanimous abandonment, and return of the multitudes show a tremendous mass concurrence in the reproductive decision-making of olive ridleys.

Within each nesting season, *arribadas* are thought to be

orchestrated by climatic and celestial events such as winds, tides, and moon phase, but the occurrence of the events often defies prediction. Frequently, *arribadas* seem to be brought about by strong offshore winds that arrive on the waning (or sometimes the waxing) quarter moon. The wind conditions make evolutionary sense in that an offshore breeze would blow the smell of turtle eggs away from land predators. But the adaptive advantages of

Two olive ridleys begin their life's journey.

nesting by a quarter moon have yet to be explained by storytelling. Because the *arribada* is believed to surprise and saturate egg predators, it makes sense that the nesting turtles benefit from some level of unpredictability, as long as they themselves could recognize and agree upon the appointed time to nest.

Among the hard-shelled sea turtles, olive ridleys are also unique for their open ocean lifestyle. Both juveniles and adults are seen at the surface over deep ocean waters. More often than not,

these turtles are found near floating logs, escaped buoys, and other drifting buoyant items. An attraction to life rafts has resulted in olive ridleys playing a role in the survival of sailors adrift at sea. In accounts such as Dougal Robertson's *Survive the Savage Sea,* sea turtles, almost certainly olive ridleys, were caught by hand as they lingered near the rafts of desperate, hungry castaways.

Conservation Status

Olive ridleys are the most abundant of the world's sea turtles, but an illusion of their unending abundance has driven mass harvests that threaten this species' existence. In modern industrial times, the olive ridley has been by far the most commercially exploited sea turtle. They remain numerous despite some drastic declines, and yet, the species' status is questionable. Like the once super-abundant (now extinct) passenger pigeon, olive ridleys may require a critical level of abundance to function as a population.

In the 1970s, approximately one million olive ridleys were taken from the waters off the Pacific coasts of Mexico and Ecuador and turned into leather goods. This pressure, in addition to extensive harvest of eggs on Pacific nesting beaches, resulted in the collapse of nearly all of the populations breeding on the beaches of Mexico. One remaining mass-nesting beach suffered severe declines, but has recently begun to recover following bans on sea turtle harvest.

In the Indian Ocean, the Orissa population of olive ridleys averages about 400,000 turtles nesting per year. However, many tens of thousands annually are drowned off these nesting beaches by fishing trawlers. In the Atlantic, the highest nesting occurs on the central north coast of South America in the Guianas, where nesting has declined 80 per cent since the 1960s.

The olive ridley is considered by IUCN to be Endangered. This status means that olive ridleys face a very high risk of extinction in the wild in the near future.

Olive ridleys grow up in the open ocean over a period of many years.

Kemp's Ridley

Scientific Name

Lepidochelys kempii.
Named for the Greek roots for 'scaly turtle' (perhaps from extra carapace scutes of the turtle's sister species) and the proper name 'Kemp' with the Latin genitive ending, from Richard M. Kemp, a fisherman who submitted the type specimen described by Harvard's Samuel Garman in 1880.

Other common names

Other English names given Kemp's ridley include Atlantic ridley, bastard ridley turtle, bastard turtle, and ridley (likely from the vernacular of fishermen, who considered the turtle's identity to be a riddle – thus, ridd-lee. Similar uncertainty about parentage brought about the term 'bastard turtle'). In Latin America, the turtle is known most often as tortuga lora.

Size and weight

Adult female Kemp's ridleys weigh between 75 and 100 lb (35 and 45 kg), with a shell straight-length of 25 to 28 in (60 to 70 cm).

Distribution

The Gulf of Mexico and warm temperate waters of the western North Atlantic, along the coast between Florida and Cape Cod, Massachusetts. Rarely in the eastern Atlantic, and unknown in the south Atlantic. Nesting occurs almost exclusively on the beaches of Tamaulipas, Mexico. Since the 1970s most Kemp's ridleys have been born in protected hatcheries in Mexico and Texas, and later released into the Gulf of Mexico.

General Appearance

As adults, Kemp's ridleys are about the weight of a large German shepherd dog. The turtle's overall coloration is olive gray above and yellowish cream underneath. Their shell is more circular than the shells of the other sea turtles and its flanged edges often make it wider than it is long. For someone who is used to seeing other more common species of sea turtles in the water, a Kemp's ridley seems unusual. The impression given by a passing Kemp's ridley is that of a ghost-like gray disk gliding by.

Kemp's ridley has a large head and a cusped parrot-like beak. Compared to the olive ridley, Kemp's ridley has a broader, less triangular head, and a flatter, broader shell. The plates covering the shell are less abundant than in the olive ridley. Kemp's ridley most often has only five pairs of lateral scutes on either side of its carapace midline and only five vertebral scutes along the midline length of its shell.

Hatchling Kemp's ridleys are dark gray all over and weigh about 1/2 oz (17 g) fresh from the nest. As hatchlings grow they develop three pronounced ridges on the middle length of their carapace and two similar ridges on the plastron. Nearing adulthood, only a thin remnant of the center carapace ridge is evident. An adult's carapace is smooth and generally un-fouled by barnacles and other opportunists.

Because Kemp's ridleys nest on dry blustery days, very little is left of their track and nest site that would allow identification. Under some circumstances, one can recognize the alternating flipper marks and narrow width – less than 25 in (65 cm) – of a ridley track leading to and from a shallow pit and low nest mound.

Adult Kemp's ridleys feed mostly on crabs and other hard-shelled animals and reach an average weight of about 90 lb (40 kg).

Distribution and Movements

Nearly all Kemp's ridleys have the same hometown beaches, those surrounding the Mexican pueblo of Rancho Nuevo, in the state of Tamaulipas. The rarity of this species and its reliance on a single basket for nearly all its eggs have raised concern

Major Nesting Beaches   Large Juveniles & Adults   Oceanic Juveniles

among sea turtle conservationists. As a result, a great deal of attention has been paid to the ridley nests at Rancho Nuevo.

Many Kemp's ridleys have had the first legs of their life's journey determined by human intervention. Since the 1970s, most have emerged from nests in protected hatcheries. Some have emerged within hatcheries near Rancho Nuevo and some have come from eggs that were transported north to hatcheries near the beaches of Padre Island, Texas, USA. Of these relocated hatchlings, some were released on Padre Island beaches only to be recaptured in the surf and taken to a sea turtle husbandry laboratory at Galveston, Texas. There, ridleys spent their formative first year in individual buckets, growing to the size of salad plates (10 in or 25 cm in shell length). After about a year, these 'headstarted' ridleys were taken from their buckets, transported by trawlers, and released offshore into the Gulf of Mexico.

Regardless of the circuitous route and helping hands that delivered young ridleys into the Gulf of Mexico, the yearling turtles are likely to spend another year or so drifting within currents. Most ridleys are found within the Gulf of Mexico and may live out their entire lives there. But many exit the gulf as juveniles and are known throughout the Atlantic coast between Florida and Cape Cod, Massachusetts. Kemp's ridleys are rarely sighted in the eastern Atlantic and they are unknown from the south Atlantic. The habitats where large juveniles and adults are typically found include turbid coastal and estuarine waters with seagrasses, mud banks, and oyster bars.

Both juveniles and adults are known to move with the seasons. Ridleys along the Atlantic coast move south as winter approaches, but turtles in the Gulf are also known to move into deeper, warmer waters as cold weather arrives. Adult female Kemp's ridleys come from the northern, southern, and eastern Gulf of Mexico to converge at their western Gulf nesting beaches.

Life History

Although biologists believe that Kemp's ridleys live near the sea surface within convergence zones, these youngest turtles are rarely observed. A rough guess is that ridleys spend one-and-a-half to two years on the open seas before they settle into shallow coastal waters.

Kemp's ridleys that leave the Gulf of Mexico were once thought to be lost. Upon further evidence, it now seems that these turtles from the eastern US coast are better able to determine their own fate than they had been credited. Yes, they are far from where they would breed as adults, but the noticeable lack of mature turtles in this wayward group would seem to indicate that they eventually depart these Atlantic waters. In fact, a continuum of small juveniles in the north and larger juveniles in the south seems to fit the story that young turtles swept out of the gulf by the Gulf Stream slowly work their way down the coast and around the peninsula of Florida.

Several Kemp's ridleys that were tagged as yearlings have been seen as adults on nesting beaches. Judging from these records and from how quickly ridleys grow, this turtle likely reaches adulthood in 10 to 15 years.

Like the olive ridley, most Kemp's ridleys breed within *arribadas*. But because of the present rarity of this turtle, the largest mass nestings involve only a few thousand turtles. The season for nesting is April through July.

An individual female is likely to nest one to three times in a season, with each nest containing approximately 100 eggs that each weighs about 1 oz (30 g). The period between successive nests is about 14 days when a turtle nests by herself but can be 30 or more days when females wait for the conditions prompting an *arribada*. It is likely that most females nest every year. Hatchlings emerge from nests in 45 to 60 days and weigh approximately 1/2 oz (17 g).

Diet

The youngest ridleys are presumed to feed on the same associates of drifting *Sargassum* that form the diet of young loggerheads. This would include a wide variety of small, slow-moving or attached organisms such as copepods, snails, and hydroids.

Larger Kemp's ridleys love to eat crabs and they seem to occupy areas where they can get the most of them. A ridley's favorite meal is the blue crab, *Callinectes sapidus*, a sprightly swimming and fast-clawed resident of secluded bay waters. Other seafood popular with Kemp's ridley includes small marine snails

Kemp's ridleys hunt blue crabs in shallow coastal waters.

and clams, and occasional jellyfish. Because balls of mud have been found in the stomachs of some ridleys, it is thought that they may take in bites of the seabottom in efforts to consume the small invertebrates hidden within.

Kemp's ridleys may also feed on the discarded bycatch from the shrimp trawlers that so commonly traverse their habitat. Stranded ridleys are commonly found to have fishes in their stomachs that are probably too fast for them to catch but are common components of the sea life tossed dead from trawl vessels.

A Kemp's ridley flings sand over her nest at Rancho Nuevo, Mexico.
Their nesting also includes bouts of rapid rocking from side to side, which produces
a distinct thumping and compacts the sand over the eggs.

Unique Traits

The largest Kemp's ridley is just small enough for a strong person to pick one up and carry it. But in doing so, one might find oneself slapped, bitten, and generally regretful for the attempt. Although Kemp's ridley is small relative to the other sea turtles, their scrappy nature makes them seem comparatively substantial.

Kemp's ridleys are fast and mean. Larry Ogren, a colleague who certainly knows ridleys better than most, has wondered aloud whether anyone would be as mean if they had to eat things that pinched their face. Certainly, having to deal with a face full of darting, slashing blue crab during every meal would favor those both nimble and determined.

The turtle does seem to have quickness beyond what most other sea turtles can show. Their disk-like shell allows a ridley to pivot on a dime and almost instantaneously change direction. In this respect they seem to be rivaled only by a green turtle of similar size.

The obstreperous nature of a ridley is easily seen in a turtle that is out of its element. Having been captured, Kemp's ridley will often thrash until exhaustion. In its attempts to deter its captors, a ridley will take every opportunity to bite them with its robust, parrot-like beak.

Kemp's ridley is also known to dance. On the nesting beach, female ridleys in the process of covering their eggs can be seen to raise their shells and rapidly thump the lower edges of their plastron against the sand. This vigorous dancing seems to be a startling departure from the way that a turtle is supposed to act. An explanation for it is that the behavior comes at a time in a turtle's nesting sequence when it might be adaptive to tamp down the sand covering her clutch of eggs. In part, ridleys may do this dance because they can. The rest of the sea turtles may be too large to lift their own weight and pull off such a routine.

Conservation Status

On a June morning in 1947, a Mexican engineer named Andres Herrera visited a beach in Tamaulipas where he and his companions stumbled upon a Kemp's ridley *arribada*. The film that Herrera made of this event stands as one of the most important clues to understanding this enigmatic species. The flickering images reveal

Presently, most Kemp's ridley hatchlings come from a single protected beach.

that Kemp's ridley was once an abundant sea turtle.

Tens of thousands of nesting ridleys were captured in time. In the film, the camera pans the stretch of coast near what is now Rancho Nuevo. What initially appears to be a boulder-strewn beach is actually a tide of turtles enveloping every available sandy space. Amidst the antics of Herrera's traveling companions stepping from turtle to turtle, it is clear that the beach was literally filled with ridleys. From the foreground to the horizon, there are turtles – crawling to and fro, throwing puffs of dry sand into the breeze, and thumping out their rocking dance moves.

The Herrera film remained unknown to biologists until 1960, when Dr. Henry Hildebrand, University of Corpus Christi, Texas, heard of the film's existence and sought out the information it contained. Upon a systematic count and careful extrapolation from the turtles visible in the film, it is estimated that 42,000 ridleys took part in that 1947 *arribada*. Only a few years after this revelation, it became clear to biologists that Kemp's ridley was in

A Turtle Excluder Device (TED) is a grid and trap door that allows turtles to escape from a shrimp trawl net.

rapid decline. By 1968, the *arribada* at Rancho Nuevo comprised only 5000 turtles, and by the 1980s, *arribadas* rarely involved more than 200 turtles. Kemp's ridley was disappearing

Years before Herrera made his film, the Rancho Nuevo ridley population was discovered by economic enterprise. Starting in the 1940s, trains of burros burdened under swollen sacks of eggs were run by *hueveros* who brought the fruits of ridley reproduction to the Mexican marketplace. For 20 years or more

the annual harvest of eggs was extensive. Recognizing this threat, the Mexican government in 1966 posted army troops at the beach to protect the ridley nests at gunpoint.

But Mexican soldiers could not guard Kemp's ridley from an even more severe threat that killed turtles before they could arrive at their beach. Following World War II, shrimp trawlers plying the Gulf of Mexico began using ever more powerful diesel engines that allowed the pulling of larger trawl nets. With the expansion of this industry, principally a fleet out of US ports, a growing expanse of shrimp habitat in the gulf was strained through the nets of trawlers.

Shrimp habitat and ridley habitat are largely one and the same. The nets that drew shrimp from the gulf also contained drowned Kemp's ridleys. By the 1960s the largest shrimp trawling effort in the world intersected perfectly with the distribution of the rarest sea turtle. For years, ridleys were known to shrimpers as a creature that clogged their nets and smashed their harvest. The incidental killing of ridleys continued for decades until roughly 1990 when shrimpers began using mandated turtle excluder devices (TEDs), which allow captured turtles to escape through a door in the net.

In the past decade or so, the future of Kemp's ridley has turned rosier. There has been an upturn in nests through the 1990s and recently the number of turtles in a single *arribada* has passed 1000. The number of nests made along Texas beaches has increased from one to two per year to dozens annually. It is uncertain whether this expansion of range is due to a general population increase, to efforts toward imprinting hatchling ridleys on Texas sands, or to both. Nonetheless, the status of Kemp's ridley remains perilous, with the world's population at only about 5000 adult females.

Kemp's ridley is considered by IUCN to be Critically Endangered. This status means that Kemp's ridleys face an extremely high risk of extinction in the wild in the immediate future.

Though still perilous, the survival outlook for the world's rarest sea turtle has improved by recent efforts to protect them.

Flatback Turtle

Scientific Name

Natator depressus.
Named with the Latin roots for a swimmer and for depressed (that is, low, which is likely to be a reference to the turtle's flattened carapace).

Other common names

Other English names given the flatback include Australian flatback and flatback seaturtle.

Size and weight

Adult female flatbacks weigh approximately 155 to 175 lb (70 to 80 kg) and have a shell length of 33 to 37 in (85 to 95 cm). Adult males are slightly smaller than females.

Distribution

Tropical marine waters between northern Australia and New Guinea. Nesting is known only from Australian beaches that are within or just outside the tropics.

General Appearance

As adults, flatbacks have the shell length of an average loggerhead but are generally only three quarters of a loggerhead's weight. Flatbacks are indeed flat. The turtle's shell is an oval with a low dome pressed downward to give a nesting turtle the appearance of being flush with the beach. The edges of the shell are depressed into flanges that upturn slightly like a hat brim. In large turtles the shell surface and edges are smooth and the turtle is generally unfettered by barnacles and other commensal growth.

The coloration of this turtle is olive gray above and cream beneath. Hatchlings are also shades of olive gray and are highlighted by bold dark outlines to their carapace scutes. A hatchling's serrated shell margins become smooth with age. The eyes of hatchlings have a turquoise glint.

At one time, flatbacks were believed to be a compressed version of a green turtle (and were placed in the same genus). Like green turtles, flatbacks have one pair of elongate prefrontal scales between the eyes and four pairs of lateral scutes on either side of the upper shell. But in addition to their low-domed appearance, flatbacks are very different from green turtles. In comparison to a green turtle, a flatback's head is much larger and triangular, and its flippers are shorter. A flatback's shell is distinctive in having thin, oily scutes that one could easily scratch through. By the time a flatback reaches adult size, the seams separating its thin carapace scutes virtually disappear, such that the shells of the oldest turtles seem covered only by skin. The flippers are distinctive in having large scales only at their margins. The remainder of each flipper is covered by supple skin with small thin scales.

Flatbacks leave tracks on their nesting beaches that look much like green turtle tracks. The turtle walks with a quick-paced butterfly gait and leaves a track of parallel flipper marks roughly a meter wide. The nest is an oval mound near a circular pit.

Distribution and Movements

This sea turtle comes closest to being endemic. It is thought that all nesting of flatbacks occurs in Australia and that many of these turtles live their entire lives in Australian waters. The complete range of the flatback stretches no farther northeast than Papua

Adult flatback turtles feed mostly on soft-bodied animals like sea cucumbers and reach an average weight of about 165 lb (75 kg).

New Guinea, no farther northwest than the eastern Indonesian islands near Timor, and no farther south than the warmest temperate waters of Australia. Flatbacks are most common on the Arafura Shelf in Tropical Australia. The turtle prefers shallow, turbid waters with soft seabottom away from coral reefs.

■ *Major Nesting Beaches*   ■ *Juveniles & Adults*

Because of their limited range, it would seem as if flatbacks don't travel much. However, it is likely that flatbacks ready to breed often find themselves hundreds of miles away from their nesting beach. Nesting migrations between foraging areas and beaches are known to span well over 600 miles (1000 km), although these trips are not likely to take turtles far from land or over deep waters. Like most of the other sea turtles, tagging studies have shown biologists that flatbacks are faithful both to their nesting beaches and to their foraging grounds.

Being sea turtles, it is astounding that flatbacks disperse as little as they do. In each of the other sea turtles, the initial scatter of young turtles within open-ocean currents ensures that they see a great deal more of the world than their own backyard. In flatback turtles, this oceanic stage is evidently lacking in their lives (see the discussion on life history below).

Life History

In the other sea turtles, much of their mysterious lives remains elusive because of the remoteness of the open ocean. But in the flatback turtle, mysteries are concealed within the turbid waters off the wild north Australian tropics.

Only recently did clues arise indicating that newborn flatbacks, unlike every other sea turtle, stayed close to land within shallow shelf waters. A principal clue came as biologists recognized pieces of hand-sized flatbacks beneath the feeding stations of white-bellied sea eagles, a raptor that seldom strays far from shore. Although sightings and strandings of flatbacks remain rare, turtles of every size are known from the same region. Age at maturity is only a guess for flatbacks, but based on limited growth information, they are likely to reach adulthood only after 20 years or more.

The absence of an oceanic dispersal stage explains why flatbacks are so restricted in their distribution. In order to bypass this stage, flatback hatchlings are substantially larger than all other hatchling sea turtles except the leatherback. At 1 1/2 oz (40 g), a flatback hatchling is nearly half again as large as a green turtle hatchling. A larger hatchling means that flatbacks are able to outsize the bites of coastal predators and reach the size for bottom feeding more quickly.

The flatback nesting season reaches peak activity during the austral summer between November and December. A female will lay an average of 50 billiard ball-sized eggs in each nest.

*Flatback turtles nest almost exclusively on the beaches
of northern Australia. They are unique among sea turtles in having
hatchlings that remain relatively close to shore.*

Hatchlings emerge from the nest in about 50 to 55 days. The number of eggs in a clutch is small and the size of eggs is large compared to other sea turtles. Nesting flatbacks make an average of three nests per season and migrate to nest about once every one to three years.

This flatback returning to the sea from Crab Island, Queensland, shares its beach with crocodiles large enough to eat it.

Diet

The smallest flatbacks are believed to feed on small planktonic invertebrates that collect near the surface over the Australian continental shelf. Most of the food items chosen by larger flatbacks are mouth-sized, soft-bodied invertebrate animals.

Seafood in this category includes sea cucumbers, soft corals, bryozoans, squid, and jellyfish. Their particular fondness for sea cucumbers matches the abundance of this resource within the turtle's soft-bottomed foraging habitats.

Unique Traits

Many of the observations of flatbacks at sea are of turtles basking at the surface. On calm days a turtle may spend hours at the surface and provide appreciated perches for tired seabirds. Speaking fancifully, it may be a fondness for sun that prompts a significant number of nesting flatbacks to crawl onto beaches during the day. Although most flatbacks choose the nocturnal nesting pattern favored by most sea turtles, a small percentage labor at their reproductive task under the burning tropical sun.

Despite their turbid habitat, flatbacks may be the cleanest of all the sea turtles. Their sleek, un-fouled, barnacle-free appearance may be due to compounds they exude through their skin or that make up their thin covering of scutes.

The shell of a flatback has a greasy or waxy feel that may result from anti-fouling substances, which prevent clinging algae, barnacles, and other hangers-on from gaining a foothold on the turtle.

Conservation Status

The flatback is ensconced within a corner of the world that has remained wild and largely unaltered by industrial human beings. Like no other sea turtle, the fate of the flatback lies in the hands of a single nation. Fortunately, both the turtle's life history and the wise stewardship of the Australian people have allowed the majority of flatbacks protection within either marine parks or world heritage sites.

Owing to the turtle's inconspicuous haunts and habits, the historical abundance of flatbacks is unclear. However it is evident that at least some populations have declined. Old photographs from the early 1900s depict large numbers of flatbacks nesting on islands near the more modern settlements of central Queensland, halfway down the Great Barrier Reef. On a number of these islands today, nesting by flatbacks is rare.

For many centuries, the aboriginal peoples of Australia have consumed and used sea turtles, including the flatback. Given that this relationship has persisted so long, it seems unlikely that this subsistence harvest has had any profound effect on the risk of flatback extinction. To the aboriginal peoples, sea turtles remain not only food, but also dreamtime ancestors. Community elders have enforced rules governing this special relationship and have determined who could catch turtles and how many turtles they could take. This traditional wisdom may serve as an explanation for the common occurrence of flatbacks in areas where industrial Europeans have not displaced the indigenous inhabitants of the Australian tropics.

One relatively new threat to flatbacks is from commercial fisheries. Trawlers, which tow nets through flatback habitat to harvest prawns (shrimp), have drowned thousands of sea turtles annually, the majority of which are flatbacks. But the recent (2000) requirement for trawlers to use TEDs (Turtle Excluder Devices) is hoped to substantially reduce this threat.

The hatchlings of flatbacks are larger than those of most other sea turtles.

Flatbacks are generally well protected in Australia by the Environment Protection and Biodiversity Conservation Act of 1999. The flatback is considered by IUCN to be Data Deficient in status. This means that there is inadequate information to assess the flatback's risk of extinction. Most biologists feel that this sea turtle's limited range makes it vulnerable to habitat changes, over-exploitation, and incidental mortality from human activity.

Leatherback Turtle

Scientific Name

Dermochelys coriacea.

Named with Greek roots for leathery turtle and the Latin descriptor for leathery skin.

Other common names

Other English names given the leatherback turtle include leatherback, leatherback seaturtle, leathery turtle, trunkback, trunk turtle, and coffin-back. In Latin America, the turtle is known as canal, tinglado, baula, and tortuga laud. Many other common names vary among cultures.

Size and weight

Most adult female leatherbacks weigh 440 to 1320 lb (200 to 600 kg) and have a shell straight-length between 4 ft 9 in and 5 ft 7 in (145 and 170 cm).

Distribution

Tropical and temperate marine waters worldwide and into the sub-arctic. They have the broadest distribution of any sea turtle. They forage as far north as British Columbia, Newfoundland and the British Isles, and as far south as the Cape of Good Hope and New Zealand. Nesting occurs on beaches mostly in the tropics.

General Appearance

Foremost, leatherbacks are magnificently large. The largest leatherback known was a male weighing 2019 lb (916 kg). It was found dead on a Welsh beach open to St George's Channel between the Atlantic Ocean and the Irish Sea. The turtle had a curved carapace length of 8 ft 5 in (2.56 m) and its flippers spanned 8 ft (2.41 m) Most leatherbacks are considerably smaller, but the average female on an Atlantic nesting beach is still impressive in having a shell length of about 5 ft 3 in (1.6 m), which would put her in the 880 lb (400 kg) weight class. Pacific leatherbacks average smaller at about 4 ft 7 in (1.4 m) in shell length.

Adult leatherbacks are dark, streamlined, scaleless turtles with long, broad flippers. Their topsides are black with random white or light gray splotches, and their undersides are splotched almost equally by black and white. While on a nesting beach, the turtle's light undersides often blush to pink. But the most conspicuous dash of color a leatherback sports is an irregular pink spot at the crown of the turtle's head. Apparently, no two spots are the same exact shape.

A leatherback's body is a barrel-shape elongated into a streamlined teardrop. They are broad-shouldered beasts, with the leading edge of their teardrop torso bulging with the muscle that powers their massive fore-flippers. Seven distinct ridges extend the length of the turtle's naked carapace and fade together at the rear, which tapers into a pointed projection. Five less-distinct ridges run most of the length of the lower shell.

Both the stiff, wing-like front flippers and the broad, rudder-like rear flippers are larger in proportion to the turtle's body than in the other sea turtles. Although front flippers are highly tapered in adults, those in hatchlings are more of a paddle shape. In larger turtles, a broad web of skin connects the rear flippers to the tail. Unlike the other sea turtles, none of the leatherback's flippers has claws.

Except in the hatchlings, leatherbacks have no scales and are covered with tough, thick, rubbery skin. The turtle's head

Adult Leatherbacks eat an array of jelly-like sea animals and reach an average weight of about 880 lb (400 kg).

is large and triangular, and the mouth is without a horny beak. A leatherback's jaws are weak by sea turtle standards and the lower jaw closes within the upper jaw in a tight scissor-like manner. Leading the upper jaw, a deep notch separates two fang-like cusps, and the lower jaw ends forward with

have the only hatchlings that crawl down the beach with a simultaneous butterfly stroke.

Nesting leatherbacks also crawl with a simultaneous gait and leave a track on the beach showing clear parallel marks from both front and rear flippers. A straight central tail-drag mark is also conspicuous. The width of a leatherback track is almost always greater than 7 ft (2 m). The turtle's nest site is most often a confused array of two or more sets of mounds and pits left as the turtle turned and crawled about while covering her nest.

Distribution and Movements

Leatherbacks are dispersed throughout the world's tropical and temperate ocean waters. The turtle is distinguished in having the broadest distribution of any sea turtle or of any reptile. This extent of range is greatly expanded by the occurrence of leatherbacks in cold waters. These turtles are

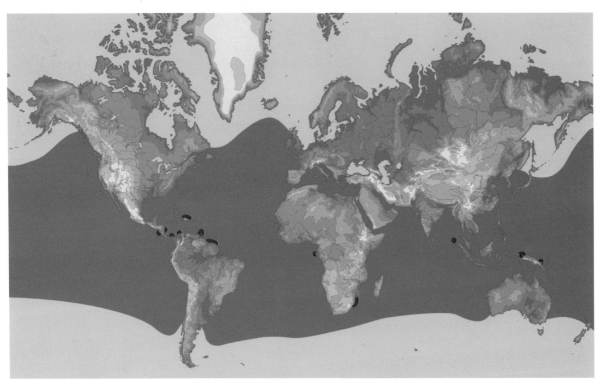

Major Nesting Beaches   Juveniles & Adults

a robust pointed hook. Leatherbacks have thick eyelids that close to a vertical slit.

Hatchling leatherbacks are black with white highlights and are covered with tiny, thin, bead-like scales. The white highlights trace the margins of the flippers, the seven longitudinal shell ridges, and an imaginary continuation of these ridges down the turtle's neck. The fore-flippers of a hatchling span one-third greater than the turtle's length, and are so large as to appear cumbersome. Of the other sea turtles, leatherbacks

known to forage as far north as British Columbia, Newfoundland, and the British Isles; and as far south as southern Chile, central Argentina, the Cape of Good Hope, and New Zealand.

The leatherback's nesting distribution is largely restricted to the tropics. Principal remaining nesting beaches are located in northern South America and the Caribbean; on Africa's Gulf of Guinea south to Angola; in the Andaman and Nicobar Islands; in Indonesia and West Papua; and on the Pacific coasts of southern

Mexico and Costa Rica. Some significant nesting occurs as far north as central Florida, USA, and as far south as South Africa. Many once important nesting areas have greatly diminished.

Leatherbacks have expansive migrations. An individual turtle might travel through the waters of both the southern Caribbean and eastern Canada in the span of only a few weeks. Once, all we knew of leatherback travels came from chance recoveries of turtles bearing stainless-steel flipper tags. But today, greater details of leatherback wanderings are revealed by the broadcasts of turtles bearing satellite radio-transmitters. This tracking has shown that in both the Atlantic and the Pacific, foraging leatherbacks wander over enormous looping paths that span entire oceans. There are some patterns to the turtles' journeys, such as high to low latitude migration preceding winter, and movement vice versa in the advance of summer, but leatherbacks are seldom faithful to geography except to nest. If foraging patterns do exist in leatherbacks, they may follow oceanographic events rather than geographical landmarks.

Like other sea turtles, leatherbacks show fidelity to their nesting beaches. Often, familiar females are seen repeatedly over many years of nesting seasons on the same small stretch of beach. Pinpoint nesting on a few miles of sand is remarkable given that leatherbacks travel many thousands of miles to get there.

Although the commutes of females are best known because we can see them at their nesting beaches, male leatherbacks are the ones best known from the coldest extent of the species' range. It is possible that females choose to limit the extent of their high-latitude wanderings during years that they return to the tropics to nest.

Life History

Leatherbacks live nearly all of their lives in waters that we generally see only from the railings of ocean-going ships. This remoteness and the turtle's recent rarity leave many questions about how leatherbacks live their lives.

A life of mysterious wanderings begins when a leatherback

A leatherback hatchling reaches wet sand during its critical crawl from nest to sea.

hatchling enters the water off its natal beach. Like older leatherbacks, young leatherbacks search for food in the open ocean. Because small turtles may have trouble diving deeply, biologists assume that neonate leatherbacks make a living near the sea surface.

Only on rare occasions are juvenile leatherbacks seen by the people desperate to study them. These juveniles are almost never observed at sea but are recovered on beaches either dead or in poor condition. In reviewing these recovery records, it was observed that juveniles up to 3 ft (1 m) in shell length came only from tropical waters. Thus, it seems that the penchant for cold water foraging begins in, and only may be possible for, leatherbacks at or near adult size.

Leatherbacks grow into adults more rapidly than other sea

chronological layers in the bones of dead leatherbacks. The research was successful in estimating ages of variously sized leatherbacks using annual rings laid down within small bony plates that encircle the pupil inside the turtle's eyeball. The technique gave an estimated age of maturity of 5 to 14 years.

If these maturity estimates are correct, leatherbacks increase in size 10,000 times in about a decade. For a reptile, this is unprecedented growth. But leatherbacks are not typical reptiles at all, as is described in the section on Unique Traits below.

Leatherback nesting reaches a peak most often during the months preceding the tropical wet season, or during what would be spring in the temperate climates of the hemisphere. Females typically lay 65 to 85 eggs in each of about four to nine nests throughout a season. Nesting events are separated by 9 to 10 day intervals. Along with the eggs in each nest, the nesting female intersperses many yolkless 'eggs' that are merely spheres of clear albumin packaged in papery eggshell. These ancillary nest

Leatherbacks nest in the tropics but may travel far to feed in productive waters near the Arctic.

turtles do. In captivity, young leatherbacks have been seen to double their weight every one to three months. Yet, a captive leatherback has never lived more than a few years and growth rates in the wild are unknown. To answer the important question of maturation in leatherbacks, George Zug with the National Museum of Natural History, USA, examined

contents, which tend to be deposited on top of the clutch, vary greatly in individual size and total number but each is normally smaller than a typical egg. The purpose of these infertile 'yolkless eggs' is widely speculated either to provide a moisture source for developing embryos, to satiate egg-predators that dig into the nest, to fill gaps between the leatherback's large eggs at the top of the clutch and prevent sand from filling the airspaces, or all of the above. They all seem like plausible explanations.

Eggs are billiard-ball-sized spheres weighing about 3 oz (76 g) and produce a hatchling weighing an average of 2 oz (44 g). Incubation periods vary greatly with temperature but most beaches have nests producing hatchlings in 55 to 70 days.

Like other sea turtles, leatherbacks may reproduce over many decades. For a female, reproduction occurs every two to three years. The reproductive habits of males are unknown.

Diet

The world's largest turtle lives and grows on a diet of clear, watery, jelly-like animals. The revelation is a bit like hearing from a champion weightlifter that they have never eaten anything but cucumbers. How could a leatherback be the biggest and grow the fastest by feeding on animals that are 96 per cent water? The answer is that leatherbacks apparently eat a lot.

Juvenile leatherbacks that have lived briefly in captivity were able to eat twice their body weight in jellyfish every day. It is possible that leatherbacks of all sizes in the wild are just as ravenous. Given the poor nutrition offered by the turtle's gelatinous food, quantity must make up for quality.

Leatherbacks are specialist feeders on slippery critters with strange names like moon jellies, cannonball jellies, and lion's mane jellies. They are also fond of similarly gooey animals like ctenophores (comb jellies), salps, and siphonophores such as the Portuguese man-o-war. Some of these menu items are spiced by stinging nematocysts potent enough to send a human to the hospital.

Leatherbacks have many adaptations that allow them to consume their squishy prey. For example, the turtle's upper jaw cusps can pierce and hold the most elusive jelly blobs. And for snacks larger than a single bite, scissor-like jaws can slice larger jellyfish – some are 18 in (0.5 m) across – into consumable pieces. Lining nearly the complete length of a leatherback's throat, rows of stiff, overlapping, 1-in (3-cm) long, cone-shaped papillae point toward the turtle's stomach. The grip of these backward-pointed spines, coupled with strong throat muscles, enable a leatherback to wring out its food and expel the excess seawater the turtle slurps in.

Unique Traits

Leatherbacks are the least turtle-like of the sea turtles. In fact, many of their traits are much more mammal-like than reptile-like.

One mammal-like trait leatherbacks have is a tendency toward being warm-blooded. To be more specific, leatherbacks are endotherms (their body heat can raise their body temperature) that remain poikilothermic (having a body temperature that varies with their surroundings). This trick is critical for an animal in need of vigorous activity while enveloped in water near 32° F (0° C). Although the turtle's body temperature varies, its internal warmth, in addition to a series of heat conservation measures, allows a leatherback to have a core temperature as much as 64° F (18° C) above the surrounding seawater.

Heat conservation measures used by leatherbacks include bundled blood vessels leading into and out of the flippers, located in the turtle's shoulders. The bundled vessels serve as counter-current heat exchange units that warm blood that has circulated through a cold flipper. The result is a conservation of heat within the organs and muscles of the trunk. The trunk is of course surrounded by a shell, which in leatherbacks is a mosaic of bone, connective tissue, and blubber-like fat lying under thick skin. Just as a marine mammal's blubber insulates in cold water, so does the fatty layer surrounding a leatherback sea turtle. Each of these thermal adaptations is enhanced by the turtle's large size. Similar to many of the larger dinosaurs, leatherbacks capitalize on gigantothermy, that is, a low ratio of their surface area to body volume (that all big animals have), which reduces the heat escaping through their skin.

A warm body opens many unique possibilities for a reptile. Leatherbacks can maintain high activity in cold surroundings, dive to chilly depths, and grow amazingly fast. These traits allow leatherbacks to perform and distribute themselves in sea-mammal-like ways. But one of the oddest turtle-mammal parallels is the leatherbacks' tendency to breech. Like the behavior seen in the great whales, leatherbacks (generally when they are

For a reptile, leatherbacks grow amazingly fast, increasing in weight by a factor of 10,000 in the span of about 10 years

perturbed by something) launch themselves vertically into the air, nearly clear the water, and come crashing down on their sides.

Conservation Status

Leatherbacks are greatly reduced from historic levels. Pacific populations, once the world's largest, are now close to being extirpated. Judging by a recent precipitous drop in nesting numbers, leatherbacks face extinction from threats that have become magnified only in the last few decades.

Before the latest declines, leatherbacks were already in trouble from threats that had taken their toll for many years. A large threat has been egg harvesting. By the 1990s, leatherback populations that once nested on the beaches of India, Sri Lanka, and Malaysia were essentially harvested to death. Today, threats more profound and insidious than egg collecting occur out in the open waters where leatherbacks forage. Chief among these is the threat from long-line fishing gear set to catch pelagic fishes such as tunas and swordfish. Leatherbacks become hooked and entangled in these lines and drown in great numbers.

Conservationists have identified long-lines as the principal reason for Pacific leatherback declines. During a time of unprecedented expansion of long-line fishing in the Pacific, the principal nesting beaches of the Pacific in Costa Rica and Mexico saw the number of visiting females drop by 90 to 99 per cent. Once, leatherbacks nesting in Mexico made up two thirds of the world's population for the species. Today, only about 1 per cent of the Mexican population remains.

Perhaps more than any other sea turtle, leatherbacks are threatened by persistent marine debris such as discarded lines and plastics. Being an open-ocean animal, leatherbacks never evolved the maneuverability needed to disentangle themselves from an obstacle. This penchant for getting tangled in things, in addition to the resemblance of plastic bags to a leatherback's favorite food, make the synthetic cast-offs of fishing activity and everyday life especially pernicious for leatherbacks.

The leatherback is considered by IUCN to be Critically Endangered. This status means that leatherbacks face an extremely high risk of extinction in the wild in the immediate future.

Leatherbacks are superlative turtles. They dive deeper, swim farther, and become larger than any other sea turtle.

Sea Turtles and Humans

Human beings have known, pondered, worshipped, and used sea turtles for many centuries. Many relationships between people and sea turtles have persisted, but many more have ended poorly for sea turtles.

Although it is romantic to think of humankind's first relationship with sea turtles as having achieved a natural balance, it is likely that as soon as we began using sea turtles, we began to use them up. Yet, in archeological evidence one finds many clues that early cultures did not take sea turtles for granted, and that these animals meant more to people than just another consumable.

Five to six thousand years ago on the Arabian Sea coast in what is now Oman, people lived with sea turtles. Remains of green turtles at many sites in this region suggest that the turtles were valued not only as food but in a spiritual context as well. Green turtles are frequently found buried in Arabian graves, often having been positioned head to head with the human occupant. Although this type of burial with animals was common through the Bronze Age in coastal Arabia, sea turtles are reported to be the most common animal used in this practice.

Continuing to the present time and throughout their global range, sea turtles have retained a spiritual value to people. Some of the mystic attributes of sea turtles seem widespread if not almost universal – representation of long life, prosperity, protection, fertility, guidance through the afterlife, general good luck, and prominence in the Earth's creation.

The most profound changes in our relationship to sea turtles came with commercial trade and the enhancement of trade by technology. One finds the most telling examples of these changes in the descriptions of Caribbean colonization by Europeans. The beginning of these colonization efforts, a cascading invasion force from Europe, came to depend on sea turtles for their very survival.

Through the sixteenth and seventeenth centuries, the Spanish, British, Dutch, and French sailed throughout the Caribbean, vied for island colonies, fought with local populations of Arawak and Carib Indians, and became very hungry. By the time that Europeans arrived in the Caribbean, much of the food providing protein to ships' crews had rotted away and the livestock familiar to continentals was ill suited for survival in the cramped holds of ships. Such a dire need for protein that could persist through lengthy sea voyages was met by the discovery of a profoundly abundant local resource – the green turtle.

Europeans discovered green turtles almost immediately upon their entry into the New World. In 1503, Christopher Columbus was toward the end of his final, disastrous voyage. Two worm-holed ships, the only remnants of a proud Spanish fleet that had left the port of Cadiz a year before, were making a desperate run from the far western Caribbean to Hispaniola and on to home. The sluggish, waterlogged vessels never made the Hispaniola port-of-call. After being blown by a tropical storm far off course to the north, Columbus found his beleaguered ships in the waters between Cuba and Jamaica and within sight of two small islands. Columbus noted that the islands were '…full of tortoises, as was all the sea about, insomuch as that they looked like little rocks…' He named the islands 'Las Tortugas' after the abundance of turtles, a name that was later changed by the British to Cayman Brac and Little Cayman, two of the three Cayman Islands.

Columbus and the remaining expedition continued on as far as Jamaica, where they were rescued after several months. Of the many discoveries heralded upon his return to Spain, tiny islands surrounded by turtles seemed insignificant. Yet, in

This olive ridley may excite European tourists, help feed a Costa Rican village with its eggs, or be worked into shoe leather in rural Ecuador.

revealing what is now thought to be the largest green turtle nesting colony ever known, Columbus began a pivotal historical role for sea turtles in the events that would shape the colonization of the wider Caribbean.

Columbus' lookout had sighted the presently known Cayman Islands on 10th May, which was probably at the beginning of the nesting season when a great annual convergence of Caribbean

The green turtle played a pivotal role in the European colonization of the Caribbean.

turtles was occurring. We can only imagine the likely scene – female green turtles, each between 220 and 440 lb (100 and 200 kg), in a sprawling aggregation filling up the shallow waters around the islands, and male-female couples bobbing at the surface in such a density as to make the sea seem like a vast field of boulders. Haphazard discovery had revealed to Europeans the hub of green turtle abundance in the Western Hemisphere -- two tiny islands that were the breeding grounds for millions of turtles.

To hungry sailors and colonials, the nesting green turtles of the

Caribbean were as profound an example of divine providence as anyone could hope for. It was a resource that could not help but be devoured. The turtles that crawled onto beaches in mass-nesting forays could be readily flipped in their tracks, carted to a ship, and stacked among the other provisions below decks. By reptilian persistence, the harvested turtles could live on their backs in a ship's hold for months, without food or water, until their butchering could yield fresh meat to a hungry crew.

The European sea captains set to the task of empire building were astounded at the limitless abundance of the Caribbean green turtle. Like the turtles' persistence as living cargo, the Cayman green turtle population seemed unending. But as provisioning turned to commerce, and as harvest turned to plunder, the deceptively abundant green turtles of the Caymans were to dwindle.

By the late seventeenth century, scores of British sloops and barques were shipping an estimated 13,000 turtles each year from the Caymans to the home Isles and to colonies elsewhere in the Caribbean. For decades during which nearly every turtle ashore was carted away, somehow, green turtle nesting on the Caymans had persisted. But in what could be predicted now but not then, the Cayman Island green turtle began a steady slide into oblivion.

One of the most important characteristics to understand about sea turtles, if we are to continue to live with them, is their time scale. Most sea turtles have a generation time that spans many decades. It is a lengthy period throughout which every turtle driven to nest on her beach might be slaughtered without any substantial evidence that the population is crashing. As decades of maturing turtles in the pipeline reach adulthood and arrive for harvest at the nesting beach, they continue to provide the illusion of an infinite resource. Just as we might continue to witness the flicker of distant stars extinguished long ago, so too can we continue to take our fill of nesting sea turtles... for a time. By the late 1700s, at a time when taste for green turtle soup at fancy British dinner parties had peaked, the Cayman nesting colony had

A farm for sea turtles. Since 1968 green turtles have undergone a process of domestication at a farm in the Cayman Islands. The effort began with adult turtles and eggs taken from Caribbean beaches outside the Caymans. The farm is now self-sufficient in that no eggs or turtles are taken from the wild to replace turtles that are either released or slaughtered for food. Those juxtaposed fates – captive turtles set free and others made into turtle burger – describe the controversial nature of the farm. It is a major tourist attraction that brings the international public into roles as both consumers of sea turtle charisma and of sea turtle meat.

Cayman farm green turtles surge toward their source of pelletized 'turtle chow.' They grow to about 4.5 pounds (2 kg) in a year and are either released into nearby Cayman waters (about 40 percent), kept on as breeding stock (about 1 percent), or grown into meat supplying local markets (about 60 percent). This demand for green turtle meat lingers in the shadow of the largest harvest of wild green turtles in history. Once, the Caymans were the breeding islands for millions of green turtles. Today, despite the release of about 30,000 farm-raised turtles since 1980, the number of female green turtles using Cayman beaches is believed to be only ten.

The olive ridley egg harvest at Ostional, Costa Rica, is a clear example of the relationship between sea turtles and humans. The harvest takes place during the first day of a multi-day arribada (mass arrival). If these first eggs were not harvested, many of them would be destroyed by the digging of nesting turtles later in the event. Some argue that the harvest removes eggs that are least likely to produce hatchlings.

Eggs harvested at Ostional are bagged, given a registered seal, and transported throughout Costa Rica. Although the eggs were historically an important protein source in the local diet, most eggs today end up in bars as an accompaniment to beer and liquor. Administered as such it is easy to imagine how the eggs have come to be regarded as an aphrodisiac. Many believe that the regulated egg harvest has minimal effects on the olive ridley population and adds incentive to protect this resource by other means. About a third of egg-sale proceeds is directed toward beach protection, research, and education. Turtle tourism also flourishes at the village of Ostional. Visitors participate in walks guided by local biologists and can be on hand when hatchlings scramble from their nests 7-8 weeks after an arribada. Although unregulated egg harvest has been implicated in the decline of many sea turtle populations, the Ostional experiment is held out as a model for sustainable use and conservation.

been essentially extirpated. Today only a handful of green turtle nests are recorded in the Cayman Islands each season.

After centuries of struggling to live on a human planet, our sea turtle species are depleted but still with us. Six of the seven extant species are threatened with extinction but none has disappeared. All over the world, sea turtles are still being consumed, but the global community has made recent progress with important international agreements to manage our consumptive relationships with sea turtles.

Apart from a continued use of sea turtles for food, adornments, and various luxury items, the most important modern threats to sea turtles come from them simply getting in our way. These threats are incidental, and mostly accidental, but they are often devastating. Foremost among these incidental threats is the capture and drowning of sea turtles by nets, lines, and hooks meant to catch fish. For most species of sea turtles, mortality from fisheries probably surpasses deaths from directed capture. For some species, especially the loggerhead, the leatherback, and Kemp's ridley, incidental mortality is by itself enough of a threat to result in extinction.

Sea turtle biologists and national governments have recognized the important role that fishery management plays in conserving sea turtles. As a result, national regulations and international agreements have begun to take reduction of sea turtle mortality into account. But the conservation task is difficult. Many of the fisheries that kill the most sea turtles, such as pelagic long-line and net fisheries for tunas and swordfish, have a high economic value and occur far from the watchful eyes of fishery managers. Thus, methods to minimize sea turtle mortality that also reduce fish catch rates are not embraced, and any enforcement of regulations is hampered by the vastness of the open oceans.

Apart from the incidental effects that we have on sea turtles, our purposeful relationship with them has begun a turn from largely predator-and-prey to substantially less harmful associations,

even to one of growing mutualism. Recently, the benefits we enjoy from living sea turtles have greatly expanded.

Some of what we receive from living sea turtles comes in the form of knowledge. Sea turtle research has yielded many recent discoveries; including how animals sense their world, migrate great distances, and live under challenging conditions. But sea turtles also leave us with many questions for the future; including how

A Kemp's ridley bound by an abandoned gill net.

they live so long, and what roles they play in our own ecology.

Humans also continue to receive spiritual and emotional benefits from living sea turtles. Many people seek them out in order to enjoy being with them. And sea turtles seem to allow this attention, at least to a limited extent; sea turtles are more approachable than most wild animals.

This approachability can be seen in the many ecotourism enterprises that feature sea turtles. Some of these allow glimpses of turtles in the water, but by far the most common tours facilitate sea turtle experiences on their nesting beaches. There, guides can bring visitors intimately close. With careful guidance, a small group of 'turtle-watch' participants can experience with all their senses an impressive wild sea animal. In these nocturnal encounters, one can taste the salt mist from the pounding surf, see the bulk of the turtle glistening in the moonlight, feel the spray of sand the turtle casts over her nest site, and hear the periodic air-rush with each labored breath, a sound that precedes the smell of low tide.

An olive ridley arrives at dusk on a Pacific beach in Costa Rica.

Even if sea turtle breath has not the smell of roses, these magnificent animals certainly embody their own brand of charisma. Almost without exception, sea turtles evoke positive emotions from people. Hatchlings are perceived as cute, swimming turtles are graceful, and all seem to amplify our sense of wonderment. Sea turtles crawl onto land where we can comfortably watch their intricate process of reproduction; but the

experiences, as spiritual ones do, leave us with more questions than answers. The turtles present themselves, only to re-enter the sea, glide away, and perform most of their astounding lives far from where we can conveniently watch.

This charisma and mystery have fostered an important mutualistic relationship between sea turtles and people. Sea turtle conservation philosophy and efforts have grown tremendously in recent decades. More than ever, programs are in place and organizations are working to understand and protect sea turtles. And this mutually beneficial relationship arrives none too soon.

In a way, one might consider the present period as being a golden age in our relationship with sea turtles. Although sea turtles have declined, our advancing technology allows us greater knowledge of them and an expanded (albeit often vicarious) familiarity with them. Even if we are never able to witness all that sea turtles do, we are able still to use our instrumentation, science, and imaging to learn from them and to share what we discover with others through a wide array of media (like this book).

Of course, sea turtles are likely to get more difficult to know the more rare they become. An intersection of lines describing disappearing sea turtles and advancing technology just may define a present-day peak in our opportunity to experience these animals. It may be that our descendants will both envy us for our capacity to experience sea turtles, and curse us for not doing more to save them. Perhaps, this golden age in our relationship with sea turtles could also be one during which a collective wisdom finds a way for this relationship to continue.

Sea turtles are mysterious and mystical, coveted and consumed. They serve us as inspiration, sentinel, commodity, and prey. Our greatest hope for a future with these animals may be in a full realization of their value and of the benefits in a world where sea turtles thrive.

INDEX
Entries in **bold** indicate pictures

RECOMMENDED READING: *The Biology of Sea Turtles*, ed Peter Lutz and John Musick, CRC Press, 1997. *The Biology of Sea Turtles*, Volume II, ed Peter Lutz, John Musick, and Jeanette Wyneken, CRC Press, 2003. *So Excellent a Fishe*, by Archie Carr, Scribner's, 1984. *The Windward Road*, by Archie Carr, University Press of Florida, 1979. *Biology and Conservation of Sea Turtles*, ed Karen Bjorndal, Smithsonian Institute Press, 1995. *Australian Sea Turtles*, by Robert Bustard, Collins, 1972. *Loggerhead Sea Turtles*, ed Alan Bolten and Blair Witherington, Smithsonian Books, 2003. *Fire in the Turtle House*, by Osha Davidson, Public Affairs, 2001. *Decline of the Sea Turtles*, by the National Research Council, National Academy Press, 1990. *Voyage of the Turtle*, by Carl Safina, Henry Holt & Co, 2006. *Sea Turtles: A Complete Guide to Their Biology, Behavior, and Conservation*, by James Spotila, Johns Hopkins University Press, 2004.

ACKNOWLEDGMENTS: I am indebted to the many friends and colleagues I've come to know through sea turtles. These include Allen Foley, Andrea Mosier, Anne Meylan, and Peter Meylan, who each provided helpful comments on the manuscript. I also thank my wife Dawn, who has contributed unique beauty to this book through her art. And for a splendidly rewarding life I thank my parents, who tempted me into a love of learning.